Graham Greene's career as a writer spanned sixty years, and he remains
one of the most widely-read novelists of the twentieth century. However, Greene's remarkable life has in recent years led to a dominance of
heavily biographical approaches to his work. *A Study in Greene* marks a
return to the literary and intellectual contexts of his writings.

In this critical study Bernard Bergonzi makes a close examination of
the language and structure of Greene's novels, and traces the obsessive motifs that recur throughout his work. Most earlier criticism was
written while Greene was still working, and was to some extent provisional, as the final shape of his *oeuvre* was not yet apparent. In this book
Bergonzi is able to take a view of Greene's whole career and argues that
the earlier work—combining melodrama, realism, and poetry—was
Greene's best, with *Brighton Rock*, a moral fable that draws on crime
fiction and Jacobean tragedy, as his masterpiece. The novels published
after the 1950s were very professional examples of skilful story-telling
but represented a decline from this high level of achievement. Bergonzi
also challenges assumptions about the nature of Greene's debt to cinema, and attempts to clarify the complexities and contradictions of his
religious ideas. Accessible and stimulating, this timely study will be of
interest to all those who enjoy Greene's novels.

Bernard Bergonzi has been Emeritus Professor of English at the Uni-
versity of Warwick since 1992, and has held visiting professorships at
Brandeis, Stanford, and Tulsa ville. Since 1961 he has published many
books of criticism and biography, and edited several more, including
Exploding English: Criticism, Theory, Culture (1990), *Wartime and Aftermath:
English Literature and its Background 1939–1960* (1993), *War Poets and Other
Subjects* (2000), and *A Victorian Wanderer: The Life of Thomas Arnold the
Younger* (2003). He has been reading Graham Greene for many years; he
still possesses the original edition of *The End of the Affair* that he bought
when

For John and Ann Rignall

A STUDY IN
GREENE:

*Graham Greene and the Art of the
Novel*

BERNARD BERGONZI

OXFORD
UNIVERSITY PRESS

OXFORD
UNIVERSITY PRESS

Great Clarendon Street, Oxford OX2 6DP

Oxford University Press is a department of the University of Oxford.
It furthers the University's objective of excellence in research, scholarship,
and education by publishing worldwide in

Oxford New York

Auckland Cape Town Dar es Salaam Hong Kong Karachi
Kuala Lumpur Madrid Melbourne Mexico City Nairobi
New Delhi Shanghai Taipei Toronto

With offices in

Argentina Austria Brazil Chile Czech Republic France Greece
Guatemala Hungary Italy Japan Poland Portugal Singapore
South Korea Switzerland Thailand Turkey Ukraine Vietnam

Oxford is a registered trade mark of Oxford University Press
in the UK and in certain other countries

Published in the United States
by Oxford University Press Inc., New York

British Library Cataloguing in Publication Data

Data available

Library of Congress Cataloging in Publication Data

Data available

Typeset by SPI Publisher Services, Pondicherry, India
Printed in Great Britain
on acid-free paper by
Clays Ltd., St Ives plc

ISBN 978-0-19-953993-2

1 3 5 7 9 10 8 6 4 2

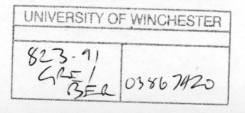

They say that's a snowflower
A man brought from Greenland.

(Graham Greene, *A Gun for Sale*)

'A novel is made up of words and characters. Are the words
well chosen and do the characters live? All the rest belongs
to literary gossip. You are not in this class to learn to be
gossip-writers.'

(Graham Greene, 'A Visit to Morin')

He searched his brain frantically. Grim-Grin he had been
ready for . . .

(Kingsley Amis, *I Like it Here*)

PREFACE

GRAHAM GREENE was a writer whose books continue to enjoy a wide readership whilst also regularly featuring in university courses. In this study I aim in the first place at general readers, in the hope that what makes sense to them will also make sense in the academy; at the same time, I pursue the critical questions that recur in academic discussions of Greene. I am assuming that readers will be familiar with the novels I discuss, and I provide only brief reminders of what goes on in them rather than detailed plot summaries. As this book is an essay rather than a thesis the scholarly apparatus is fairly light but, I hope, sufficient. Greene's books exist in a variety of editions on both sides of the Atlantic, which makes it impractical to provide sources for the many brief quotations from them. But where the quotations are long enough to be set separately I have inserted a parenthetical reference to the chapter and section of the book in which they appear. Greene's comments on his own work come from his *Ways of Escape* unless otherwise indicated. Short stories that I refer to can be found in his *Collected Stories* and essays in the *Collected Essays*. I quote Greene's film reviews from *The Pleasure Dome: The Collected Film Reviews 1935–40*, published in 1972, since it is a book I possess, but his writing on and for the cinema is more fully represented in *Mornings in the Dark: The Graham Greene Film Reader*, which came out in 1993, though it lacks the illustrations in the earlier book.

I append a list of Greene's books, indicating the dates and order of publication, but I do not supply a detailed bibliography; secondary material that I have drawn on or referred to is listed in the notes. Grateful acknowledgements are due to editors who over the years

have asked me to review books by or about Greene; to William
Thomas Hill for commissioning an essay on *Brighton Rock* for a
collection he was editing; to John Garvey for putting me on to
Shusaku Endo, and for allowing me to quote remarks about Greene
he made in a private communication; to David Lodge for his
writings, and our conversations, about Greene; and to my wife for
many things, but specifically for encouraging me to get on with
this book, and for reading and commenting on a draft of it.

B.B.

CONTENTS

Introduction

I HAVE been reading Graham Greene all my adult life—I still have the original edition of *The End of the Affair* that I bought when it appeared in 1951—and have been writing about him for many years. Some time ago I realized that I had accumulated enough essays and reviews on him and his work to make into a short book. When I went over this material, though, it was evident that it would need more attention for anything coherent to be made of it, and I was disinclined to make the effort; as much as anything because I realized that I had never properly made up my mind about aspects of Greene. Then I was provoked by the publications and discussions that marked the centenary of his birth in 2004. I disagreed with much of what was said, but it was a creative disagreement that gave me some fresh ideas and led me to write the present study, which is a new (and, I hope, original) work, though some of it draws on previously published writing. A lot of the centenary material was of a promotional kind, even if it appeared as literary journalism, acclaiming Greene as a great British novelist and a national asset, who had achieved a global reputation (and there are not many modern English writers of whom that can be said). This praise was echoed by some of Greene's co-religionists, who, after swallowing hard, acclaimed him as a great Catholic novelist.

The most substantial publication of the year was the third and final volume of Norman Sherry's huge biography of Greene, of which the first volume had come out in 1989. Since Greene's death in 1991, he has been the subject of intense biographical attention. It addition to Sherry's authorized work, there have been shorter biographies by Michael Shelden, W. J. West, and Anthony Mockler (whose promised second volume has never appeared), and memoirs by his mistress Yvonne Cloetta, and his friends Leopoldo Durán and Shirley Hazzard.[1] This material is interesting and informative, but it feeds the insatiable English appetite for literary biography. I have nothing against biography, indeed, I have perpetrated it myself, but one can have too much of a good thing. Reading works of imaginative literature can be demanding, and reading biography is usually easier. There is a danger of substituting the life for the work as an object of attention, in a way that reinvigorates the venerable Romantic doctrine that reading literature is one way of encountering the soul of a great man (and it is usually a man), while reading his life-story is another way. Greene's long life easily lends itself to delving into personality: there was his manic-depressive temperament, his rakish good looks, his idiosyncratic attachment to Catholicism, which made him at one time much preoccupied with Hell, his several serious affairs and many brief sexual encounters, his incessant travels in later years to exotic and sometimes dangerous parts of the world, the secret service work which he was engaged on in the Second World War and intermittently continued afterwards. Greene could well have been a character in a novel himself, which is rather how Sherry treats him. Indeed, after his death a scathing picture of him appeared in John Banville's novel *The Untouchable*. It is, I believe, a serious defect of Sherry's biography, particularly its final volume, that he tends to collapse Greene's novels back into their sources, so that the fiction is merely an epiphenomenon flickering above the life. A reviewer of Cloetta's memoir produced a sentimental, watered-down version of the Romantic 'great soul' doctrine when she wrote, 'Greene, like V. S. Naipaul and unlike, say, Anthony Powell or Trollope, is a writer whom one longs to have known personally. His novels seem so intensely intimate that one yearns to have a larger piece of him.'[2] Such excesses confirmed my growing conviction that it is time to leave off studying Greene's life, of which we now know more than enough, and return to his writing; for, in short, criticism rather than biography. There have been a number of critical studies of Greene's work, some of them very good, such as the one by Kenneth Allott and Miriam Ferris in the 1950s, and Roger Sharrock's in the 1980s.[3] Most critics were writing while Greene was still alive and working; the final shape of his career was not yet apparent and assessments were still somewhat provisional. Now that Greene is among the illustrious dead his oeuvre is complete and can be read and interpreted as a totality, like that of other eminent twentieth-century novelists, such as E. M. Forster or Virginia Woolf or Ford Madox Ford.

Greene was himself an excellent critic, particularly of authors for whom he felt an affinity, like Dickens and Henry James. Greene's essay 'The Young Dickens' is a good example. In the course of it he remarks, 'It is a mistake to think of *Oliver Twist* as a realistic story: only late in his career did Dickens learn to write realistically of human beings'. This passing comment anticipates my own approach to Greene. So does the opening of his essay 'Henry James: The Private Universe': 'The technical qualities of Henry James's novels have been so often and so satisfactorily explored, notably by Mr Percy Lubbock, that perhaps I may be forgiven for ignoring James as the fully conscious craftsman in order to trace the instinctive, the poetic writer back to the source of his fantasies.' Greene could be an acute critic of his own work, as he shows in the introductions to the collected edition, which later appeared in his second volume of autobiography, *Ways of Escape*. But Greene as auto-critic needs to be read cautiously. In *Ways of Escape* he gave a balanced account of his novels and entertainments of the 1930s, showing that he still thought well of some of them, particularly *Brighton Rock*. But in his collected conversations with Marie-Françoise Allain, *The Other Man*, he was dismissive: 'Today my early novels horrify me, they're so absurd. There's nothing worse than poetic prose.'[4] Once, Greene had used 'poetic' as a term of praise in his literary essays and film reviews, and it applies to his earlier novels. Novelists, like anyone else, have the right to change their minds, but there were times in Greene's later life when he seemed to be denying, or at least rewriting, his past. I take Allain's book, illuminating as it sometimes is, with reserve. In life Greene was a notorious practical joker and leg-puller, and in interviews he tended to say what he thought was expected of him, or sometimes what would provoke the interviewer. In 1953 two interviewers asked him what influence Mauriac had on his work. Greene responded that there had been very little. The interviewers then tried to trump him by saying, 'But you told Kenneth Allott, who quotes it in his book about you, that Mauriac had a distinct influence.' Greene's reply was unabashed, 'Did I? That is the sort of thing one says under pressure.'[5]

Greene may have been reclusive in his life, disliking critics and would-be biographers (though he reluctantly honoured his agreement with Sherry), but in his autobiographical writings and in interviews he scattered *obiter dicta* about his life and work which have become familiar. There are the recurring motifs from his early life, the revolver in the corner cupboard and the green baize door, and the influence of Marjorie Bowen's novel *The Viper of Milan*, where Greene found what he called his 'pattern': 'perfect evil walking the world where perfect good can never walk again, and only the pendulum ensures that after all in the end justice is done'. Another literary reference which Greene invoked is from Browning's 'Bishop Blougram's Apology':

> Our interest's on the dangerous edge of things.
> The honest thief, the tender murderer,
> The superstitious atheist, demirep
> That loves and saves her soul in new French books—
> We watch while these in equilibrium keep
> The giddy line midway.

These lines reflect the atmosphere of Greene's novels from the middle 1950s onwards, where moral opposites tend to merge or exist in uneasy equilibrium. It is no longer a world where perfect evil walks the world or can even be identified, though in 'The Young Dickens', which is dated 1950, he refers to 'the eternal and alluring taint of the Manichee, with its simple and terrible explanation of our plight, how the world was made by Satan and not by God, lulling us with the music of despair'. Such passages indicate different phases of Greene's work, which I go on to discuss. I quote them now simply to indicate how readers have readily followed Greene's hints and suggestions in interpreting his work; this tendency has been reinforced by the recent heavy waves of biography, which swallow up the work in the life. My aim is sometimes to read against the authorial grain, looking at the texts in their own terms, recalling Eliot's belief in the separation between the man who suffers and the mind which creates, and Lawrence's insistence that one should trust the tale, not the artist. I employ the close reading associated with the old New Criticism that I grew up with, and the scarcely less antique classical structuralism that I frequented in the 1980s; readers should be warned that this is a work of old-fashioned criticism. At the same time I am drawn to later approaches that emphasize intertextuality, the ways in which literature draws on other literature, a relevant consideration with a writer as well read as Greene. A degree of biographical context and continuity is inescapable, and I am admittedly interested in the religious and political ideas at work in his oeuvre, but the emphasis will be on what he did with them. The 'Greene' I refer to will be the 'second self', in Edward Dowden's phrase, the figure who emerges from his writings, rather than from the laundry lists and dirty linen uncovered by biographers. Chesterton once wrote that it is the business of the critic to uncover things that the author was not aware of and may not have wanted to know: 'Either criticism is no good at all (a very defensible position) or else criticism means saying about an author the very things that would have made him jump out of his boots.'[6] More recently Frank Kermode, in his essay 'Secrets and Narrative Sequence', has pointed out that there is more to reading a literary narrative than following the story: 'Secrets, in short, are at odds with sequence . . . and a passion for sequence may result in the suppression of the secret. But it is there, and one way one can find the secret is to look for suppression of evidence, which will sometimes tell us where the suppressed secret is located.'[7] One can try to locate the secrets without immediately reconnecting the text to the life. Allott and Ferris made an acute comment in *The Art of Graham Greene*: 'In reading Greene's novels and entertainments it may be more useful to think of the structure of *The Duchess of Malfi* than that of *Barchester Towers* or *The Newcomes*.'[8] That study appeared in 1951, before even *The End of the Affair*, and the body of work it examined showed Greene at his most poetic as well as his most melodramatic. Greene thought highly of Webster, particularly of *The Duchess of Malfi*, and he is closer in temperament to him than to Trollope or Thackeray.

To return to the centenary discussions. Reviewing Sherry, Mark Lawson remarked on the way Greene's novels were rather short compared with many of his contemporaries': 'Greene's brevity was the combined result of reaching artistic maturity during war-time paper-rationing and an ability to write sentences with a much longer shadow than their size suggested.'[9] The concluding assessment is correct and well put, but it is preceded by errors and an implication I strongly dispute. The novels that Greene wrote before the war were all short, shorter indeed than some of his later ones; his brevity was there from the beginning and had nothing to do with wartime paper-rationing, which in any case affected the number of books that could be printed rather than their size. More significant is the suggestion that Greene did not reach artistic maturity until the 1940s, which is, in effect, to dismiss much of his best writing. In the 1940s, in the middle of his Catholic phase, Greene changed the nature of his fiction. It is evident from recent responses that many writers now assume, like Lawson, that the later work is what matters. This is true of Zadie Smith, in an essay on *The Quiet American*.[10] It is the first and best of the quasi-political novels that Greene embarked on in the 1950s and it deserves its fame. Smith gives an intelligent account of the book, though she is too ready to take Greene's pronouncements on his life and writing at face value; she praises the novel for its documentary truth, and remarks, 'Too much time has been spent defending Greene against the taint of journalism; we should think of him instead as the greatest journalist there ever was.' Perhaps; but once he had been a kind of poet. Another centenary critic, Julian Evans, sees Greene as a moralist whose interest is essentially 'on the dangerous edge of things': 'he carries with him the odour of a moral ambiguity unpalatable to our piously moralizing, hypocritical times. We are drawn to him as a model, but cannot bear too much of his morality.'[11] This is clearly meant as high praise, but it is hard to construe.

As I have said, such disagreements have given me a clearer sense of what I regard as Greene's achievement as a writer of fiction. He was often described in the centenary commemorations as a 'great writer', and here my dissent is clear-cut. The word 'great' is commonly devalued in promotional discussion. (I am reminded of Gerard Manley Hopkins's complaint, 'This is a barbarous business of greatest this and supreme that that Swinburne and others practise.'[12]) Nevertheless, I think it is worth trying to redeem. I believe that for a male novelist to be regarded as 'great', a necessary but not a sufficient reason is the ability to create lifelike and convincing female characters; one thinks of Emma Bovary, Anna Karenina, Isobel Archer, Molly Bloom. Greene, whose women tended to be recurring types, lacked this capacity; except in *The End of the Affair*, which is unlike any of his other novels. There Sarah Miles is a living presence, and by all accounts she was closely based on Greene's lover Catherine Walston. If Greene was not a great novelist he was certainly a very good one, which should be sufficient acclaim, though I shall complicate the picture by suggesting that in his best work he was not a conventional novelist either. My aim in this study, which puts it in opposition to much current opinion, is to shift the focus of attention back to the first phase of his work. I believe that the novels and 'entertainments' up to and including *The End of the Affair* are what Greene most deserves to be remembered for, even allowing for elements that are immature and unconvincing. In those books he draws on a wide range of literary and generic sources: traditional adventure stories, contemporary thrillers, the cinema, medieval morality plays, Elizabethan and Jacobean drama. In one aspect they are intensely realistic, casting a cold but intent eye on urban life in early twentieth-century England, recording its transformation by technology and mass culture of largely American origin. Nevertheless, for all the realistic observation, I believe that in this phase he was not attempting to produce what Roland Barthes called the 'classic realist text'. How to describe what he wrote then is not easy; one can use words such as 'romance' or 'fable',

8

but they are very approximate. One can, though, call it poetic, in ways suggested by the comparison with Webster. The early novels are richly and sometimes extravagantly metaphorical in language. Their characters tend to be types or archetypes, caricatures or grotesques. At this time Greene was interested in the old drama, which presented the embodied abstractions of virtues and vices rather than characters in the modern sense. He sees these elements surviving in Shakespeare even while they are being transformed into 'character': 'Here is the watershed between the morality and the play of character: the tension between the two is perfectly kept: there is dialectical perfection. After Shakespeare, character—which was to have its dramatic triumphs—won a too-costly victory.'[13] These remarks have their relevance for Greene's earlier practice of fiction, where 'character' is subordinated to other ends. The process culminates in *Brighton Rock*, which is packed with precise observations of the seaside resort, the holiday crowds, the pubs, cinemas, dance-halls, racecourses. It is a suspenseful crime story and at the same time the first of Greene's Catholic novels, which presents a moral fable about damnation. The teenage gangster Pinkie is far more than a juvenile delinquent; he is presented as a demonic figure of extraordinary power and cruelty.

For a long time I believed that *Brighton Rock* was Greene's best novel of the 1930s; now I am convinced that it is his finest work. Nevertheless, I try to discuss his whole long career as fairly as possible, though I do tend to believe that some books are better than others. My focus is on the novels, though I make occasional cross-references to Greene's short fiction and his plays.

The title of this book, *A Study in Greene*, echoes the first of Arthur Conan Doyle's Sherlock Holmes stories, 'A Study in Scarlet'. As I show in the first chapter, among the 'secrets' as opposed to the 'sequence' of Greene's writing was his interest in colours, particularly in things that were green, and people called Green or Greene. In a simple sign-system, such as traffic lights, the opposite of green is red, and Greene liked giving his female characters names that are derived from red, like Coral, Ruby, and Rose. No one is called Scarlet, though, and the closest we come is in *It's a Battlefield*, where a laughing girl brushes past Conrad Drover: 'He looked after her, but she was already out of sight, a piece of scarlet material vanishing into the interior of a bus.' Greene thought highly of Conan Doyle, praising the 'poetic quality' of the Sherlock Holmes stories in an essay on him, so he might have appreciated the link and the implied tribute.

NOTES

1. Norman Sherry, *The Life of Graham Greene*, 3 vols. (London, 1989–2004); Anthony Mockler, *Graham Greene: Three Lives* (Arbroath, 1994); Michael Shelden, *Graham Greene: The Man Within* (London, 1994); W. J. West, *The Quest for Graham Greene* (London, 1997); Leopoldo Durán, *Graham Greene: Friend and Brother* (London, 1994); Shirley Hazzard, *Greene on Capri* (London, 2000); Yvonne Cloetta, *In Search of a Beginning: My Life with Graham Greene* (London, 2004).

2. *Times Literary Supplement*, 19 September 2004.

3. Kenneth Allott and Miriam Ferris, *The Art of Graham Greene* (London, 1951); Roger Sharrock, *Saints, Sinners and Comedians: The Novels of Graham Greene* (Tunbridge Wells, 1984).

4. Marie-Françoise Allain, *The Other Man: Conversations with Graham Greene* (Harmondsworth, 1984), 131.

5. Martin Shuttleworth and Simon Raven, 'The Art of Fiction: Graham Greene', in Samuel Hynes (ed.), *Graham Greene: A Collection of Critical Essays* (Englewood Cliffs, NJ, 1973).

6. In an essay on *The Old Curiosity Shop* in *Criticisms and Appreciations of Charles Dickens*, 1911.

7. Frank Kermode, *Pieces of My Mind: Writings 1958 – 2002.* (London, 2003), 105.

8. Allott and Ferris, *Art of Graham Greene*, 32–3.

9. *The Tablet*, 9 October 2004.

10. *Guardian*, 18 September 2004.

11. Julian Evans, 'Graham Greene', *Prospect*, September 2004.

12. *Further Letters of Gerard Manley Hopkins*, ed. C.C. Abbott (London, 1970), 246.

13. Graham Greene, *British Dramatists* (London, 1942), 19.

I

Obsessions and Jokes

IN 1929 Graham Greene hit the ground running in the opening paragraph of his first novel, *The Man Within*:

He came over the top of the down as the last light failed and could almost have cried with relief at the sight of the wood below. He longed to fling himself down on the short stubby grass and stare at it, the dark comforting shadow which he had hardly hoped to see. Thus only could he cure the stitch in his side, which grew and grew with the jolt, jolt of his stumble down hill. The absence of the cold wind from the sea that had buffeted him for the last half hour seemed like a puff of warm air on his face, as he dropped below the level of the sky. As though the wood were a door swinging on a great hinge, a shadow moved up towards him, and the grass under his feet changed from gold to green, to purple and last to a dull grey. Then night came. (ch. 1)

The prose may be rather too careful and deliberate, but it effectively conveys physical sensations; this is in every sense a promising opening for a young novelist who was not yet 25. *The Man Within* is a historical novel set among Sussex smugglers in the early years of the nineteenth century. The running man, Francis Andrews, is the son of a smuggler, now dead. He has been brought up in his father's gang but has betrayed them to the authorities, in a gesture which seems as much an act of filial independence as a desire to uphold the law. Andrews's action is an early instance of the preoccupation with betrayal that runs through Greene's work, and which his autobiographical excursions and the researches of biographers have traced to childhood experience. Andrews is the first of many figures in Greene's fiction who are literally or figuratively on the run. He has acknowledged the early influence of the adventure stories that are written for boys but often enjoyed by men. He admired his distant kinsman R. L. Stevenson; and *Kidnapped*, a great story about a man on the run, was an evident influence on *The Man Within*, though the large sweep of Highland scenery is reduced to the small-scale landscape of the Sussex Downs. In 1938, reviewing a poor film version of Stevenson's novel, Greene complained, 'All the great filmic scenes of battle and flight are eliminated'; he tried to achieve such 'filmic scenes' in his own first novel.[1]

In *The Man Within* Andrews falls in love with Elizabeth, a 19-year-old girl who is beautiful, ethereal, and virginal; but he also has a sexual encounter with Lucy, the comfortably carnal mistress of the lawyer Sir Henry Merriman. Such an opposition between female types is a recurring motif in Greene; in his first novel it appears as the traditional Catholic duality of Madonna and Magdalen. It may reflect a division in Greene, who for many years was devoted to his wife Vivien, a madonna-like figure by all accounts, whilst regularly frequenting prostitutes. In his subsequent novels there is a contrast between a good-time girl (or older woman) who is sexually active and a frail, immature, waif-like female who seems virginal even if she is technically not so: Kay Rimmer and her sister Milly in *It's a Battlefield*, or Ida and Rose in *Brighton Rock*.

At the end of *The Man Within* Andrews and Elizabeth commit suicide, as do a succession of characters in Greene's novels and plays. His characters run a high risk of being killed off at the end, all the way from *The Man Within* to his last novel, *The Captain and the Enemy*. Early in the novel Andrews reflects, 'It was only to suit his own ends or his own self-pity that he allowed himself the pleasure of melodrama'. *The Man Within* is a melodramatic tale that culminates in a *Liebestod*, and Greene shared his character's taste for the pleasure of melodrama. In 1953 he said in an interview, 'melodrama is one of my working tools and it enables me to obtain effects that would be unobtainable otherwise, but on the other hand I am not deliberately melodramatic'.[2]

There are anticipations of Greene's later writing in *The Man Within*, such as the potting shed behind Elizabeth's cottage where Andrews takes refuge, which was to provide the name and central symbol of a play. Subtler, and more interesting, are those moments when Andrews, *in extremis*, sounds like Greene's later creations. ' "For years," Andrews said, "I've longed for a peace, a certainty, a sanity."' This is close to Scobie's troubled thoughts as he contemplates suicide in *The Heart of the Matter*: 'I've longed for peace and I'm never going to know peace again.' To take another instance: 'Andrews suddenly sat down at the table and buried his face in his hands. Oh God, he prayed silently, if you are God give me courage. Don't let me start all over again by betraying her. I thought I'd won out of this cowardice at last.' In the last lines of *The End of the Affair* Maurice Bendrix addresses God in similar tones, though with a different import: 'O God, You've done enough. You've robbed me of enough, I'm too old and tired to learn to love, leave me alone forever.' What these anticipations—or echoes—indicate is that the unconscious forgets nothing, and when Greene was presenting emotional situations that were important to him he was likely to draw on forms of expression, words, or intonations that he had used long before and had probably forgotten about. Another passage in *The Man Within* signals some of Greene's major preoccupations. There is a gripping scene in which Andrews tries to elude his pursuers by hiding in a wood, with a thick mist all around: 'He began to think that he could distinguish sounds. Several times he imagined his own name.' Years later, Querry, the central character of *A Burnt Out Case*, hears a voice coming from

OBSESSIONS AND JOKES

the Congo jungle: 'Somebody is calling out there. I thought for a moment it was my name. But one always seems to hear one's own name, whatever anyone really calls.' In *The Comedians* Brown, the narrator, dreams that he is being called: 'Someone called out sharply behind me, "Brown, Brown," but I was not certain whether that was my name or not, for I didn't turn. "Brown". This time I awoke and a voice came up to me from the veranda below my room.' Names, and his own name in particular, were always of great importance to Greene, as Philip Stratford showed in a valuable article, which I have freely drawn on in this chapter.[3]

In *The Lawless Roads* Greene describes how when he was travelling in Mexico in 1938 he was fascinated to discover a town where many of the inhabitants were called 'Greene' or 'Graham', though entirely Mexican in nationality and culture. He began to be oppressed by his namesakes: 'one found oneself haunted by fantasies, as if fate intended to take in its octopus coils yet another Greene.' He describes how the local chief of police promised to introduce him to one of the indigenous Greenes:

The chief of police had—forcibly—kept his promise and summoned a rather scared Greene to see me in the police station. His name was De Witt Greene; he had Dutch, American, English, and pure Indian blood in him, for his grandfather, who had come from Pennsylvania after the Civil War, had married a cacique's daughter. His great-grandfather had come from England. As we walked across the plaza together he had pointed—'There's another Greene'—at a seedy Mexican, with a drooping hat and a gun on his hip, descending the Treasury steps. (ch. 6)

The last sentence shows an early use by Greene of the adjective 'seedy', so often applied to his world by critics. Greene appends a footnote to this passage: 'The other day, reading in d'Urfey's anthology *Pills to Purge Melancholy* (1720), I came across a Mr Witt Greene, the author and composer of a formal Restoration song— "Never Sigh but Think of Kissing". Certainly family migration may be a daunting thing.' In *British Dramatists*, Greene acknowledged an earlier literary namesake, the playwright Robert Greene. After dismissing some minor Elizabethans, he adds, 'To Greene alone perhaps is this judgment a little unfair: Greene with his idealised milk maids, cool-fingered, spiritual and content, who ranged the air above the dreary room, the alehouse and the stews which formed his actual scene—a scene perhaps more pleasing to scholars than to men who live those lives.'[4] He may be implying that Robert Greene presents an ideal world and Graham Greene the actual one. In his article Stratford quotes other examples of the novelist's interest in literary or historical figures called Greene or Green. He notes that in 1956 Greene wanted to visit a remote frontier province in India where a rebellion was taking place. His reason was that the leader of the rebels was reportedly called Graham Greene, but the Indian government did not think that a good enough reason to grant him an entry permit. Sherry has recorded how in his later years Greene was troubled by a mysterious figure who kept intervening in his life and claimed to be called 'Graham Greene'.

It is not clear how Greene knew that the Mexican Greenes did in fact spell their names with a final 'e', but he took the difference seriously; it was a way of distinguishing him from other writers who used the more common form, such as Henry Green, F. L. Green, and Julian Green. There is a parallel in his play *The Living Room*, where the members of the Browne family are proud of the final 'e'. In nature green and brown often go together, and several of Greene's characters are Browns: Pinkie in *Brighton Rock*; the protagonist of *No Man's Land*, a film treatment that Greene wrote as a novella in the early 1950s and was published in book form in 2005; and the central figure in *The Comedians*; while in *The Captain and the Enemy* the eponymous Captain, who goes through life under many different names, confesses that his name had originally been Brown. In the same novel the narrator, suddenly needing to invent the name of an imaginary friend, comes up with Browne. (In *The Human Factor* a passer-by is identified as 'Browne, with an e'.) Greene avoided using his own surname (or Green) for his characters, though the fleeing murderer in *Stamboul Train* is called 'Grünlich', which means 'greenish', and the Victorian philosopher T. H. Green has a small part in Greene's radio play *The Great Jowett*. His one-act play of 1980, *Yes and No*, presents the rehearsals for a new play by a famous dramatist called Privett, an unmistakably greenish name. Stratford claims that though Greene avoids the proper name, he frequently refers to green things in his writing. He does not engage in any statistical analysis, and I remain cautious, for many things in the world are likely to be green. But the 'green baize door' is a recurring motif in Greene's writing, derived from the door dividing the school where his father was headmaster from the adjoining family home, though its greenness is not the most important thing about this significant barrier. I must acknowledge that on opening *The Confidential Agent* at random I came across the sentence, 'The trouble with Conway is he won't touch greens.' And a reference in *A Gun for Sale* looks deliberate. Greene disliked the phrase 'Greeneland', but in that novel, published in 1936, before he was well known enough for it to have become a critical cliché, he invoked the actual country. A girl plays a gramophone record of a popular song, and Greene provides the lyrics (as he did in several of his novels of the 1930s):[*]

> They say that's a snowflower
> A man brought from Greenland,
> I say it's the lightness, the coolness, the whiteness
> Of your hand.

As I have remarked, Greene shows an implicit concern with greenness in his choice of names for girls or women that suggest

***

* See Bergonzi, *Reading the Thirties* (London, 1978).

its chromatic opposite. There is Coral Musker in *Stamboul Train*, and Coral Fellows in *The Power and the Glory*, Ruby in *A Gun for Sale*, and a whole bunch of Roses. The first of them is a minor character in *It's a Battlefield*, Rose Coney. In that novel the disturbed Conrad Drover goes to buy a dozen saffron roses as a present for his sister-in-law. Then, 'When he was half a mile away he saw they had given him pink roses'. He is angrily disappointed and unsuccessfully tries to throw them away. We never know why he does not want pink roses. Subsequent Roses are younger. A Rose Higginbotham is fleetingly mentioned in *A Gun for Sale*. Rose Wilson in *Brighton Rock* is linked chromatically and maritally with Pinkie Brown. She is followed by Rose Cullen in *The Confidential Agent*, and Rose Pemberton in *The Potting Shed*. Rose Cullen dislikes her name: 'but then, you see, my father's crazy about roses'. In *Travels with my Aunt*, Henry Pulling's Aunt Augusta tells him, 'Your father once said to me, "The first girl I ever slept with was called Rose. Oddly enough she worked in a flower shop."' In Greene's earlier work one is not sure how far the echoes and repetitions are deliberate, but by 1969, when he published *Travels with my Aunt*, he was writing in a vein of conscious self-reference. This novel contains the fourth cremation in his fiction, and makes rather heavy-handed allusions to *Stamboul Train* and *Brighton Rock*. In *Monsignor Quixote* there are reminders of *The Power and the Glory*.

The personal name that Greene drew on most frequently was one he never used publicly. He had been christened Henry Graham, which was the name he appeared under in a walk-on part in a François Truffaut film of 1972, *La Nuit Américaine* (*Day for Night* is the English title); he had previously considered publishing *The Confidential Agent* under the pseudonym 'Henry Gough'. Sir Henry Merriman, the pompous lawyer in *The Man Within*, is the first of a succession of Henrys in Greene's fiction and drama. There is the suicide Henry Scobie in *The Heart of the Matter*, the cuckold Henry Miles in *The End of the Affair*, and the globe-trotting retired bank manager Henry Pulling in *Travels with my Aunt*. There are off-stage Henrys in two of Greene's plays: Henry Callifer in *The Potting Shed* and Henry Tomlinson, another cuckold, in *Carving a Statue*. In *May We Borrow Your Husband?*, a slim collection of short stories published in 1967, four different Henrys are mentioned, and there are fleeting appearances of the name in other works. When Greene visited the Congo in 1959, gathering material for *A Burnt Out Case*, he noticed with interest that one of the local people was called Henry, and spelt his name with a 'y' although it was a French-speaking area. In these references we see an obsession turning into a joke, at least for the author and those of his readers who might pick it up. Greene was a notorious practical joker, who sent spoof letters to the press under a variety of pseudonyms, including 'Henry Ash' and 'Mrs Henry Montgomery'. Once he entered a *New Statesman* competition for a parody of his work and won second prize. Greene's jokes with names are private but not altogether inaccessible, given a certain amount of biographical information. One of them, however, remained obscure for a long time. In *The Confidential Agent*, D., on the run from his enemies, takes refuge in an empty London flat; the name by the bell is 'Glover'. This was inexplicable until Greene's biographer revealed that at that time he had a mistress called Dorothy Glover. Other parallels and repetitions remain puzzling. There is, for instance, no obvious reason why the principal male and female characters in both *The End of the Affair* and *The Human Factor* should be named Maurice and Sarah. One has to allow for the possibility that Greene, who did not like rereading his work, had simply forgotten that he had already used those names.

Greene turned obsessions into jokes, perhaps as a means of controlling them. In 1980 he took this process as far as it could go, in *Doctor Fisher of Geneva or the Bomb Party*, a weird, dream-like fantasy. Doctor Fisher is a monster, a Swiss millionaire who is vicious and totally cynical. He manipulates the world around him in a parody of divine providence, embodying the idea of the novelist-as-joker, which had long fascinated Greene.

If Greene ever had an *alter ego* he might have been called Henry Brown. Jokes and private references provide a strand of unity in his large fictional oeuvre, signalling the presence of the hidden author. Greene's critics have been very ready to find a deeper unity in the persistence of the themes of betrayal and lost innocence, notwithstanding the wide range of social and geographical settings. Roger Sharrock has referred to a 'fresh disguise for the single novel he is writing all the time', and remarks, 'Greene's obsessional, almost neurotic drive constantly reasserts itself so that it is nearer to the truth to express change as a reshuffling of the cards, not the introduction of a new pack'[5]. This is a persuasive comment, but my emphasis in this study is different. In this opening chapter I have taken a brief bird's-eye view of the oeuvre, or more technically made a spatial or synchronic reading, tracing the recurrence of motifs and preoccupations. Such descriptive analysis can be illuminating but it only takes one so far. Despite the recurring elements, I believe that there are important discontinuities and fresh starts in Greene's literary career, and in this study I attempt to examine them and the questions of comparative value that they raise. In doing so I pay less attention to Greene's obsessions and recurring themes than to the ways in which he wrote about them.

NOTES

1. Graham Greene, *The Pleasure Dome: The Collected Film Criticism*, ed. J. R. Taylor (London, 1972), 197.

2. M. Shuttleworth and S. Raven, 'The Art of Fiction', in S. Hynes (ed.), *Graham Greene* (Eaglewood Cliffs, NJ, 1973), 165–6.

3. Philip Stratford, 'Unlocking the Potting Shed', *Kenyon Review*, 24 (1962), 129–43.

4. Graham Greene, *British Dramatists* (London, 1942), 13.

5. R. Sharrock, *Saints, Sinners and Comedians* (Tunbridge Wells, 1984), 130, 258.

2

Into the Thirties

GREENE was reported to have been annoyed when John le Carré described him as a man of the 1930s. It would be understandable if he thought that his literary significance should not be restricted to the first ten years of a career that covered sixty. But they were extraordinarily productive years: if Greene had died at the end of the decade he would be on record as the author of eight novels, a collection of short stories, and two travel books. There were also many literary essays and film reviews, later collected, and a biography that remained unpublished until the 1970s. The patterns of thought and feeling in his work, the things he was moved by and curious about, had affinities with other writing of the 1930s, in the work of the so-called Auden generation. Though much of the Victorian order had survived, despite the devastations and dissolution caused by the First World War and the subsequent industrial depression, English life was increasingly affected by an expanding mass culture, often American in origin. The traditional face of England was marked by cinemas and roadhouses, petrol stations, new motor roads, and spreading suburbia. Greene was keenly interested in these innovations. He did not always like them but he did not recoil from them in horror as D. H. Lawrence or George Orwell did, and he incorporated them into his fiction. One of the key cultural phenomena of the late 1930s was the movement known as Mass Observation, in which teams of volunteers submitted reports on what they did and what they saw on a particular day, in an attempt to provide a cross-section of national consciousness. Greene's fiction of the 1930s shows something of this sociological curiosity, and one of the characters in his last novel of the decade, *The Confidential Agent*, the Indian Mr Muckerji, is a keen mass-observer.

Greene's pre-war novels manifest the nervous energy that enabled him to write so much in so short a time, and though they are sometimes implausible in plot and situation they present what I regard as a satisfying thickness of texture. This is not the language we generally use in discussing fiction, but I believe that at that time Greene was not writing conventional novels. As Allott and Ferris argue, they resembled Jacobean dramas rather than the established masterpieces of Victorian fiction. Michael Shelden, a perceptive critic though a hostile biographer, takes a similar approach when he says: 'In the first half of his career Greene played down the importance of creating plausible characters and plots. For him the crucial elements in his novels were the same as those in a dramatic poem.'[1] Greene's novels of the 1930s draw on the contemporary popular culture of films and thrillers, as well as older writers of adventure stories and historical romance, such as Stevenson, Rider Haggard, and John Buchan. There are, too, extensive reminders of earlier poets and dramatists. (Greene, though he left Oxford with a second-class degree in history, was much better read in English literature than many academics who are now paid to teach it.) He combined these various elements with a serious concern with the art of fiction, where his mentor was Henry James. At that time 'poetic' was a strong word of approbation for Greene, which he applied to Dickens and James and Conan Doyle. Some of his most interesting film criticism reflects on the nature of 'poetic cinema': 'not plays by Shakespeare adapted to a medium even less suitable than the modern stage; but poetry expressed in images which let in a little more of common life than is in the story'.[2] K. W. Gransden, in an illuminating article, asked, 'is not Greene the most poetic of living English prose writers?'[3]

The Man Within did remarkably well for a first novel. It was a critical success—Aldous Huxley preferred it to Virginia Woolf's latest—and sold 8,000 copies. On the strength of that Greene gave up his job as a subeditor on *The Times* and became a professional writer. But the success was not repeated by his second and third novels, *The Name of Action* and *Rumour at Nightfall*. They deal respectively with political intrigue in the Rhineland, which Greene had briefly visited in the 1920s, and the Carlist wars in nineteenth-century Spain, though, as he later confessed, 'I knew next to nothing of Spain where the story takes place (at sixteen I had spent one day between Vigo and Coruña).' They sold badly and Greene later ejected them from his canon: 'Both books are of a badness beyond the power of criticism properly to evoke—the prose flat and stilted and in the case of *Rumour at Nightfall* pretentious (the young writer had obviously been reading again and alas! admiring Conrad's worst novel, *The Arrow of Gold*), the characterization non-existent.' Greene ensured that the books would never be reprinted in his lifetime, a prohibition now laid upon his literary estate, which means that they will be inaccessible until 2061. They can be consulted only in copyright libraries, which is where the present writer once read them (long ago, in fact, he briefly owned one of them, which he had found in a second-hand shop and sold for far too little). In practical terms these books are unavailable for critical discussion. So, having acknowledged their existence, I shall say no more about them.

The failure of these books meant that Greene's career was in crisis. Everything depended on his next novel, *Stamboul Train*; here, finally, he directs his attention at contemporary English life; or at least a small segment of it travelling across Europe from Ostend to

Constantinople (as Istanbul was still known) as passengers on the Orient Express. Greene observed, 'for the first and last time in my life I deliberately set out to write a book to please, one which with luck might be made into a film. The devil looks after his own and in *Stamboul Train* I succeeded in both aims.' The film was not made for some time, but the novel was well enough received for it to be the choice of the English Book Society, which revived Greene's fortunes for a while. Greene follows a fictional formula that was popular in the early 1930s: a cosmopolitan and heterogeneous collection of people come together in the arbitrary confines of a luxury hotel or an international express train. Agatha Christie's *Murder on the Orient Express*, published a year after Greene's novel, is a classic detective novel using this formula (the American edition of *Stamboul Train* was called *Orient Express*). David Lodge has written of *Stamboul Train*, 'the structural device that weaves these diverse strands together, involving the characters wittingly or unwittingly in each other's destinies, is the journey itself. Time and place are marked by the progress of the train between the various stations on its route, which supplies the title of the novel.'[4] Greene's travellers are mostly English and not very glamorous, and there are not many of them, though he deploys them skilfully. The lesser ones run to caricature, such as the peevish middle-aged couple who are continually complaining, or an absurd clergyman who is on his way to become chaplain at the British embassy in Budapest. There is the ace reporter Mabel Warren, a familiar type in the popular culture of the time, though she adds something to the model by being a mannish-looking lesbian travelling with a conventionally attractive female companion, Janet Pardoe. Observing the other travellers is the popular novelist Mr Q. C. Savory, who takes pains to emphasize his plebeian origins; this bit of characterization brought Greene into trouble; the popular novelist J. B. Priestley claimed it was based on him and threatened to sue for libel. Twenty pages had to be rewritten and reprinted at Greene's expense. His liking for types and caricatures was a matter of inclination rather than incompetent characterization. He wrote of his admiration for the types in medieval morality plays or Ben Jonson's comedy of humours.

The principal figures in *Stamboul Train* are more complex, like Carleton Myatt, a prosperous young businessman. He is travelling to Istanbul in pursuit of his interests in the currant trade. Myatt is a Jew and is frequently referred to as such, which has caused Shelden to condemn Greene for his anti-Semitism. There is no doubt that Greene was mildly anti-Semitic, if in an unthinking way, since it was the default position of large areas of English cultural and intellectual life before the advent of Hitler and the Second World War. After that Greene, like many people, changed. One sign of the change is a modification of the references to Jews in *Brighton Rock*. Myatt is not, in fact, a stock anti-Semitic caricature; at a moment of crisis, when the train is held up in the Balkans, he reflects in a chillingly prophetic fashion, 'It was in some such barren quarter of the world, among frozen fields and thin cattle, one might expect to find old hatreds the world was outgrowing still alive.' There is a brief romantic encounter between Myatt and Carol Musker. She is one of Greene's recurring types: the girl who is minimally attractive, frail, waif-like, and vulnerable, but always plucky (to use an almost obsolete adjective). Lisa, in Greene's last novel, *The Captain and the Enemy*, shows the persistence of the type. Coral is a dancer on her way to join a troupe in Constantinople. She does not know very much about the world, but she knows how to look after herself, which includes adopting an American accent, as favoured in the showbiz milieu where she is trying to make a living.

Love makes a momentary appearance in *Stamboul Train*, and politics a more emphatic one. Among the passengers is Dr Richard Czinner, a Yugoslav Communist who has been in exile in England

and is now returning to his native land to lead a revolution. The attempt fails, and in a scene of melodramatic violence at a wayside station he is killed before he reaches Belgrade. Nor does Coral, who has become fortuitously caught up with Czinner, ever get to Constantinople. She is taken up by Mabel Warren, whom Janet has left, and is driven back to Vienna in a hired car. The political dimension faintly anticipates the concerns of Greene's later fiction, though it is very vague on points of detail. Czinner has been brought up as a Catholic, which would make him a Croat, though his name is Hungarian, not implausible in that country of mixed populations. But it is unlikely that a Croat would lead a revolution in the Serbian capital. Nevertheless, the vaguely sketched-in rising anticipates the actual socialist revolution in Vienna two years later.

Stamboul Train contains various basic elements of popular fiction: exotic settings, love interest, comedy, excitement, and crime. The last of these is provided by Josef Grünlich, who boards the train at Vienna when he is fleeing from the murder he has committed in the course of a burglary. Yet all these elements of plot are subordinated to the fact of the journey itself: the movement of the train and the unfolding of the narrative go together. As Shelden puts it, 'a constant procession of sharp images helps to convey the sensation of hurtling across Europe on an old steam express in winter'; *Stamboul Train* 'seems to be as much a long poem as a novel'.[5] The sharp images are evident in the novel's finely evocative opening paragraph:

The purser took the last landing-card in his hand and watched the passengers cross the grey wet quay, over a wilderness of rails and points, round the corners of abandoned trucks. They went with coat-collars turned up and hunched shoulders; on the tables in the long coaches lamps were lit and glowed through the rain like a chain of blue beads. A giant crane swept and descended, and the clatter of the winch drowned for the moment the pervading sounds of water, water falling from the overcast sky, water washing against the sides of channel steamer and quay. It was half past four in the afternoon.

The passage shows the poetry of precise observation. It is also intensely cinematic, suggesting the 'poetic cinema' which Greene favoured in his film reviews. The cinematic dimension of his art is important, though not always properly understood, and I shall return to it shortly. It is worth noting that the poetry of this opening paragraph is of a comparatively traditional kind, the *'poésie des départs'*, which pervaded the imagination of the late nineteenth century. As Lodge has remarked, 'the railroad train is one of the few products of the industrial revolution to have acquired a certain mythic quality'[6]; one thinks of the train journeys in Dickens and Hardy, Tolstoy and Dostoevsky, and of paintings by Frith and Monet. Early in the twentieth century Arthur Honegger expressed this mythic quality in music, in his tone-poem about a locomotive, *Pacific 231*; to keep his imagination charged, Greene continually played a gramophone record of it while he was writing *Stamboul Train*. The frontiers which the train crosses are a result of the First World War (and contained in themselves many of the causes of the Second). But Dr Czinner, a Marxist, has a sense of the future and of contemporary technology. He tells the Yugoslav officers who are interrogating him: 'How old-fashioned you are with your frontiers and your patriotism. The aeroplane doesn't know a frontier; even your financiers don't recognize frontiers.' A few years later Greene was writing novels in which aeroplanes and international financiers play an important part.

The popular novelist, Mr Savory, is another character who is aware of one of the transforming cultural forces of the twentieth century, as he observes the passing landscape from the train: 'One thing the films had taught the eye, Savory thought, the beauty of landscape in motion, how a church tower moved behind and above the trees, how it dipped and soared with the uneven human stride, the loveliness of a chimney rising towards a cloud and sinking behind the further cowls.' Savory is a rather absurd figure and treated mockingly, but here Greene seems to be writing out of his own experience. He was interested in the cinema from his undergraduate days onward and was involved with it for much of his life; between 1935 and 1940 as a film critic for the *Spectator* and *Night and Day*, and subsequently as a scriptwriter and, briefly, as a director. His writings about film have been conveniently collected in *Mornings in the Dark: The Graham Greene Film Reader*, edited by David Parkinson (1993). It is well known that Greene's fiction presents sharply visual effects and that these can be described in cinematic terms: close-ups, long shots, panning sequences, the alternations and juxtapositions of montage. It has therefore been widely assumed that Greene got all these things from the film and that he was one of the first novelists to have been influenced by cinematic technique. The claim is crudely made in a quotation from *Newsweek* that appears on recent paperback editions of Greene's novels: 'A master storyteller, one of the first to write in cinematic style with razor-sharp images moving with kinetic force'. Parts of Greene's novels were indeed written in 'cinematic style'; but then so were novels written well before the cinema was invented. Greene acknowledged as much when he referred to 'the great filmic scenes of battle and flight' in Stevenson's *Kidnapped*. One can indeed argue that Greene gets his effects from the cinema. But if one then asks, 'where did the cinema get its effects from?', the only possible answer is, 'from the nineteenth-century novel'. The loop runs back to literature. There is much evidence for this, particularly in the writings of the great Russian director Sergei Eisenstein. In *Film Form* he describes how the pioneers of cinema, like himself and D. W. Griffith, had access to an invention with extraordinary powers and possibilities, but they had to work out what to do with it if they wanted to tell stories. To learn how to construct cinematic narrative they turned to existing literary forms, primarily the novel, but looking back as far as classical epic. In Eisenstein's words, 'The pages of literature offer us models of completely unexpected compositional structures, in which are presented phenomena that "in themselves" are quite ordinary.'[7] Eisenstein begins his essay 'Dickens, Griffith and the Film Today' with the boiling kettle that opens Dickens's *The Cricket on the Hearth*: '"The kettle began it!" But, strange as it seems, movies were also boiling in that kettle. From here, from Dickens, from the Victorian novel, stem the first shoots of American film esthetic, forever linked with the name of David Wark Griffith.' Eisenstein goes on to show how much Griffith discovered about the making of films in the novels of Dickens, which he had always loved. Eisenstein himself, in a brilliant demonstration of Dickens's cinematic possibilities, sets out a long passage from *Oliver Twist* in the form of a shooting-script, to which it is perfectly adapted. The passage describes early morning on the streets of London, with a welter of dense anarchic life beginning to fill them. It is aurally as well as visually responsive, responding to 'the whistling of drovers, the barking of dogs, the bellowing and plunging of oxen, the bleating of sheep, the grunting and squeaking of pigs, the cries of hawkers, and shouts, oaths and quarrelling on all sides, the ringing of bells, and roar of voices that issued from every public house.' This was something that the early, silent cinema could not reproduce. Dickens was, of course, an intense visualizer, and not all novelists were, but he is far from alone in his cinematic qualities. Thomas Hardy is another writer whose work can be seen in a filmic fashion, as Lodge has shown in an interesting essay, 'Thomas Hardy as a Cinematic Novelist'.[8] Conrad is a further examplar. *The Secret Agent*, which Greene confesses he read not wisely but too well when he was writing *It's a Battlefield*, is full of cinematic effects. There is the powerful scene in which Winnie Verloc, having realized that her husband was responsible for her young brother's death, takes a carving knife and stabs him as he is lying on a sofa: 'He was lying on his back and staring upwards. He saw partly on the ceiling and partly on the wall the moving shadow of an arm with a clenched hand holding a carving knife. It flickered up and down. Its movements were leisurely. They were leisurely enough for Mr Verloc to recognize the limb and the weapon.' After the murder, as Mrs Verloc sits numbly pondering, she becomes aware of a steady ticking sound, far too loud to be the clock in the room. She looks towards the body and notices

a flat object of bone which protruded a little beyond the edge of the sofa. It was the handle of the domestic carving knife with nothing strange about it but its position at right angles to Mr Verloc's waistcoat and the fact that something dripped from it. Dark drops fell on the floorcloth one after another like the pulse of an insane clock. At its highest speed this ticking changed into a continuous sound of trickling.

It is a compelling example of cinematic writing, done at a time when film narrative was still in its infancy. The 'camera' shows us what Winnie—and the reader—sees as she looks for the source of the ticking. The passage anticipates not only the visual devices of the film but the aural ones, and Conrad was writing twenty years before the advent of the talkies. The chapter ends with a lingering shot of a trivial object: 'Mrs Verloc on reaching the door had stopped. A round hat disclosed in the middle of the floor by the moving of the table rocked slightly on its crown in the wind of her flight.' It is the kind of effect we are used to calling 'Hitchcockian'. (Hitchcock was a director whom Greene disapproved of, though he was given to using such devices in his own fiction.)

Critics who notice such scenes and episodes in the realistic novel tend to call them 'anticipations' of cinema, of a quirky or mysterious kind. Leon Edel, discussing Balzac's cinematic qualities, remarks, 'We feel as if that massive "realist" had a prevision of the cinema.' This is rather like saying a man 'anticipates' or has a 'prevision' of his children's appearance. Eisenstein emphasized the genetic model:

it is always pleasing to recognize again and again the fact that our cinema is not altogether without parents and without pedigree, without a past, without the traditions and rich cultural heritage of the past epochs. It is only very thoughtless and presumptuous people who can erect laws and an esthetic for cinema, proceeding from premises of some incredible virgin-birth of this art!

Returning to Greene, I hope to have established that the idea of him being 'one of the first to write in cinematic style' is nonsense. Nevertheless, one can acknowledge that his familiarity with films sharpened his perceptions, and that his understanding of film technique gave him a fresh insight into problems of narrative composition. In his earlier novels, up to and including *The Power and the Glory*, Greene created powerful visual effects, and it is surprising that in 1959 he wrote of himself that he had very little visual imagination; it may have been a quality that declined over the years.[9] On occasion Greene seems to have taken material from his film reviews into his fiction. For instance, at a tense moment in *A Gun for Sale* we read:

He could hear the slight shuffle of cinders where the two were walking; it wasn't easy to follow them because of the sound his own feet made. They disappeared round a stationary truck and the light failed more and more. He caught a glimpse of their moving shadows and then an engine hooted and belched a grey plume of steam round him; for a moment it was like walking in a mountain fog. A warm dirty spray settled on his face; when he was clear he had lost them. (ch. 4, 2)

In a film review published in November 1935, when he was writing *A Gun for Sale*, Greene wrote: '*Sous les Toits de Paris* contained a sequence in which Préjean was surrounded by a gang with drawn razors in the darkness of a railway viaduct; the smoke blew contin-ually across, and the dialogue was drowned in the din of shunting trucks. The steamy obscurity, the whispers, the uproar overhead combined to make the scene vividly sinister.'[10] The atmosphere is very similar, even if the points of detail are different. In 1936, reviewing *Rose of the Rancho*, Greene commented witheringly on the male lead: 'I find Mr Boles, his air of confident carnality, the lick of shiny black hair across the plump white waste of face, peculiarly unsympathetic.' This description reappears in *Brighton Rock* (part 6, 2).

Greene, for all his familiarity with cinema, remained deeply literary in his points of reference; his film reviews make recurring references to the modern writers who were important to him—James, Conrad, Ford Madox Ford—as well as to the older dramatists: Marlowe, Ben Jonson, Webster, Dryden. A reference to Flaubert is particularly significant. The 'agricultural show' episode in *Madame Bovary* is a major innovation in the development of fictional narrative. In this scene Rodolphe directs amorous advances at Emma while in the background a public official delivers a pompous speech about the importance of agriculture, and prizes are awarded to local citizens for their produce and livestock Two modes of discourse are harshly interwoven. The effect is irresistibly comic, though Flaubert's purpose was to show how romantic feeling was impossible in the gross, materialistic nineteenth century:

He took her hand, and she did not withdraw it.
'General Prize!' cried the Chairman.
'Just now, for instance when I came to call on you . . .'
'Monsieur Bizet of Quincampoix'
'. . . how could I know that I should escort you here?'
'Seventy francs!'
'And I've stayed with you, because I couldn't tear myself away, though I've tried a hundred times.'
'Manure!'
'And so I'd stay tonight and tomorrow and every day for all the rest of my life.'

'To Monsieur Caron of Argueil, a Gold Medal!'
'For I have never been so utterly charmed with anyone before.'
'To Monsieur Bain of Givry St Martin'
'And so I shall cherish the memory of you.'
'For a merino ram . . .' (Translated by Alan Russell, Harmondsworth, 1979, 161–2)

Eisenstein refers to this episode in *Film Form* as a literary device that was to be of great importance in cinematic narrative: 'it was Flaubert who gave us one of the finest examples of cross-montage of dialogues, used with the same intention of expressive sharpening of idea'.[11] Greene invokes it (a little inaccurately: it was a prize-giving, not an auction) in discussing the French directors he admired: 'French directors at their best have always known the trick of presenting a more intimate reality: the horrible or the comic situation—in the hands of Duvivier or Clair—is made convincing, by its careful background of ordinary life going on, just as Madame Bovary's furious passion was caught up in the dust and cries of the cattle auction.'[12] The 'cross-montage of dialogues' has now become commonplace in both films and novels. Its possibilities were much enlarged by the advent of radio, which enabled a disembodied and potentially dissonant voice to be inserted into a scene. There is a good example in *A Gun for Sale*. Raven, the man on the run, is hiding, tired and scared, in a suburban garage. From the neighbouring house he uncomprehendingly hears a broadcast reading of extracts from Tennyson's *Maud*. The dominant radio is a feature of the ultra-modern hotel in *The Confidential Agent*: 'Music came up from Luxemburg, Stuttgart and Hilversum: radio was installed everywhere. Warsaw suffered from atmospherics, and National gave a talk on the Problem of Indo-China.' The last detail suggests Greene's famous proleptic power. In 1939, when the novel was published, there was no obvious problem of Indo-China (later Vietnam), but when *The Quiet American* appeared in 1954 it had become pressing.

The moderate success of *Stamboul Train* encouraged Greene to persevere with a literary career. Like his previous novels, it was published without any subtitle, but a later edition was described as 'an entertainment' after Greene devised the distinction between 'novels' and 'entertainments'. The idea seems to have been to direct readers with undemanding tastes to the 'entertainments', which would be closer to popular fiction, with elements of melodrama and the fast-moving thriller. These qualities, though, are not dominant in *Stamboul Train*, and Greene seems merely to have wanted to emphasize that it was a good read. Later, though, he came to think of the 'entertainment' as a specific genre of his own fiction, and published several novels which were described as such. Eventually Greene came to regard the distinction as factitious, and he abandoned it for the Collected Edition.

It's a Battlefield was emphatically a novel, of a serious and carefully plotted kind. It received a warm review from V. S. Pritchett, and, as Greene puts it, 'a kind word from Ezra Pound and some words of praise from Ford Madox Ford'. Otherwise, though, it did not arouse great interest, and has since been consistently underrated. After the late nineteenth-century undertow and romantic setting of *Stamboul Train, It's a Battlefield* is a work of contemporary realism, which takes place almost entirely in the London of the early 1930s. It is beautifully written, closely observing the life of the streets, and giving it a poetic intensity. After the episodic unfolding of the previous novel, this one has a strong central situation, and a dominant central theme. It observes the classical unities of time, space and action, taking place over a few days in central or suburban London, apart from a brief excursion into what was then rural Hertfordshire. At the heart of the narrative, though he barely appears as a character, is Jim Drover, a Communist bus driver who is in prison under sentence of death. In the course of a scuffle at a political demonstration he has stabbed and killed a policeman, though he claimed he was trying to protect his wife from an attack. He has been found guilty of murder and an appeal has been turned down; he is to be executed in a few days, but there is rising political unrest about his case, and the Home Secretary has his own reasons for considering a reprieve. Jim's wife Milly is one of Greene's plucky waifs, while his brother Conrad has risen out of the working class via scholarships to become chief clerk in an insurance office. He is a lonely, insecure man who has long been in love with Milly. Kay Rimmer, Milly's sister, lives with her in Battersea. She works in a match factory and is, in the language of the period, a cheerfully promiscuous good-time girl. (Her surname has obscene implications to present-day ears; I rather doubt if they were current in 1934, but if they had been Greene might not have worried.) Lesser characters include Mr Surrogate, a vain and wealthy Communist intellectual. Kay goes to bed with him, and with Jules, a young Anglo-French waiter in a Soho restaurant, of whom she is genuinely fond. On the edge of the action is the curious personality of Conder, a crime reporter always looking for a story. He is a fantasist, who talks continually about his large family, though in fact he is unmarried, living alone in a room in Soho, devoted to his collection of foreign money. Set apart from these characters, though involved in their lives in many respects, is the unnamed Assistant Commissioner of the Metropolitan Police.

As a fictional character the Assistant Commissioner is central to the story, and at the same time deeply flawed. He is closely derived from the Assistant Commissioner in Conrad's *The Secret Agent*. Both men are known only by their title, with their names never indicated; both have served in a tropical colony and are not really at ease with desk work. They have a 'hands-on' attitude to practical policing and involve themselves in it, to the resentment of their subordinates. Greene was well aware of his excessive debt to Conrad's novel (which in places approaches plagiarism: in both novels the

Assistant Commissioner meets a smooth young man who is private secretary to the Home Secretary, and who is trying to shield his master from worries). Conrad's policeman is a subtler and stronger character than Greene's; Conrad makes his appointment to such a senior post after colonial service seem at least plausible, which Greene does not. But having embarked on *It's a Battlefield*, he could not remove the Assistant Commissioner, though he resolved to give up reading Conrad for a long time to come. At one point, when he was revising the novel, Greene attempted to drop the episode in which the Assistant Commissioner insists on joining the policemen who are going to arrest an armed murderer. It is unconvincing in the context of the plot, though it is a powerful piece of writing. In the event Greene found that the story needed this episode and he had to keep it.

The Assistant Commissioner is indeed a necessary figure. He has no beliefs about justice or politics, but he tries to be a fair and efficient policeman. He is an alienated but loyal servant of the state, an early version of the weary professionals who appear in Greene's later novels; he looks back longingly at his life in the jungle, among so-called savages. This sentiment was to become prominent in Greene, though when he wrote *It's a Battlefield* he had not yet made his first visit to West Africa, which he described in *Journey Without Maps*. The Assistant Commissioner is distracted from proper policing because the Home Secretary wants him to report on the likely public response to a reprieve for Jim Drover, a matter on which the policeman has no opinions himself. He is a keen observer of the urban scene and spends a lot of time watching it as he walks the streets of London, like Inspector Bucket in *Bleak House*. He is *spectator ab extra*, and his thoughts function like a chorus privately commenting on the action. It is via the Assistant Commissioner that Greene presents the theme indicated by the novel's title, and the epigraph from the historian A. W. Kinglake. This describes the

Battle of Inkerman in the Crimean War, which was fought in fog: 'In such conditions, each separate gathering of English soldiery went on fighting its own little battle in happy and advantageous ignorance of the general state of the action.' The idea of modern urban society as a jungle or a battlefield is far from original, but in Greene's novel the metaphor is given historical backing. The First World War is a recent memory, and there is already talk and fear of another war, like the one Evelyn Waugh had outlined with relish at the end of *Vile Bodies*. The novel is rich in metaphor, and many of them have a military reference; ' "No," he said, "No. You must take care of yourself. There's still hope". The words were bundles of grenades flung into her parapet.' The Assistant Commissioner reflects, 'the little glass rooms along the passages at Scotland Yard were like the deep dug-outs of an intricate trench system. He couldn't ask a question without troubling some inspector's self-importance.' And later, 'He was like a general left alone at head-quarters to study the reports from every unit; they littered his desk. But he was not sheltered in a château behind miles of torn country; the front line was only a hundred yards away, where the trams screamed down the Embankment and the buses circled Trafalgar Square.' The Assistant Commissioner has served in the war, so it is natural for him to think in such terms. But Greene boldly uses such imagery to convey the sensations of characters who have not had such experience. Milly, trying to think about her husband in his prison cell, recalls how close they had been: 'But now, because she could not imagine his surroundings, could not tell whether he was awake or asleep, communication was barred. Although they loved each other, their minds were like two countries at war, with the telegraph wires down and the rails torn up.' This is not how Milly would have thought of things, but Greene makes effective use of the technique of 'free indirect style', which enables the author to move in and out of his character's consciousness.

It's a Battlefield is a poetic novel. This is evident in its metaphorical energy, and what Roger Sharrock calls the 'urban poetry' of the imagistic, intensely evocative presentations of the London scene in the early 1930s:

The man who tears paper patterns and the male soprano were performing before the pit queues, the shutters of the shops had all gone up, the prostitutes were moving west. The feature pictures had come on the second time at the super cinemas, and the taxi ranks were melting and re-forming. In the Café Français in Little Compton Street a man at the counter served two coffees and sold a packet of 'Weights'. The match factory in Battersea pounded out the last ten thousand boxes, working overtime. The cars in the Oxford Street fun-fair rattled and bounced, and the evening papers went to press for the last edition—'The Streatham Rape and Murder. Latest Developments'. 'Mr MacDonald Flies to Lossiemouth'. 'Disarmament Conference Adjourns', 'Special Service for Footballers', 'Family of Insured Couple Draw £10,000. Insure Today'. At each station on the Outer Circle a train stopped every two minutes. (ch. 1)

One can if one likes call such a passage 'cinematic', but if it is, it is cinematic in the manner of Dickens's account of London street life as cited by Eisenstein. Greene is in fact writing in a tradition of novelistic presentation of the city, whether Dickens's London, Balzac's Paris, or Joyce's Dublin. At the same time, there are features that place it in its period, noted in a Mass Observing fashion. The cinema was becoming a dominant feature of English life, as described by Greene in his novels and by many other contemporary writers. Kay Rimmer, at work in her factory, links herself to the superstars of the age: 'Norma, Greta, Marlene, Kay'. The newspapers, represented by their headlines, were not new, but by the early twentieth century the press had become popular, competitive, and strident. Some of these headlines provide motifs that recur throughout the novel. The 'Streatham Rape and Murder' is one of the cases that the Assistant Commissioner resents being distracted from by the Drover enquiry. The news that the Prime Minister, Ramsay

Macdonald, was travelling by air to his Scottish birth place, imparts a further note of modernity. The final sentence of the passage contains one of Greene's sly interventions. The Assistant Commissioner has visited the prison where Drover is awaiting execution: 'This was not the worst pain, hope and fear in a cell, visits from the Chaplain; he had a dim memory that someone had once mapped hell in circles, and as the searchlight swooped and touched and passed, and the bell ceased clanging for Block C to go to their cells, he thought, "this is only the outer circle".' The Assistant Commissioner's dim memory is of Dante's *Inferno*; the idea of the 'outer circle' is picked up by Greene's reference to trains on the Outer Circle stopping every two minutes. In fact there has never been a part of the London Underground called the Outer Circle. What is now known as the Circle Line used to be called the Inner Circle, in reference to a plan, long abandoned, to construct an outer one. Greene liked setting up these slightly laboured parallels and echoes, as when the prison in which Jim Drover is confined is presented as resembling the match factory where his sister-in-law Kay works.

It's a Battlefield is poetic in its imagistic precision, and in its wealth of metaphor and simile. Some critics have insisted on a difference between these two devices, claiming that metaphor presents a fusion of two references, whereas simile, seen as a lower form, merely relates them. This is not a distinction I accept, since I see simile as a more explicit form of metaphor; both devices show one thing in terms of another, for the purposes of expanding meaning or establishing a significant contrast. Greene was much given to simile in his fiction of the 1930s and 1940s. In later years, though, he turned against what he saw as his earlier metaphorical excesses. He told Marie-Françoise Allain, 'My first books were very bad, full of metaphors which I chose for their extravagance, influenced as I was by my readings in the twenties, when I was very attached to the

English Metaphysical poets of the seventeenth century, who devoted themselves to highly complex rhetorical exercises.'[13] I believe that Greene had more immediate fictional sources for his taste for metaphor than the Metaphysical poets, in the novelists whose influence he acknowledged, Stevenson, Conrad, and James. Gransden has referred to the wide range of similes in *Kidnapped*, the book that heavily influenced Greene's first novel. Some of them are simply descriptive, but others contain depths of implication, and one on the last page reverses abstract and concrete in a way that looks very typical of Greene: 'there was a cold gnawing in my inside like a remorse for something wrong'. Henry James, in the later work, was given to startlingly elaborate similes. There is a good example in 'The Turn of the Screw', a work which Greene greatly admired, and imitated in his painful early story 'The End of the Party'. The narrating governess is becoming more and more confused and distressed, and her state of mind is indicated in a simile: 'The summer had turned, the summer had gone; the autumn had dropped upon Bly and had blown out half our lights. The place, with its grey sky and withered garlands, its bared spaces and scattered dead leaves, was like a theatre after the performance—all strewn with crumpled playbills.' The shift from natural to artificial is startling and revealing. One sees why Greene had referred to James as a poet, and had hoped to achieve such effects in his own prose.

One has to admit that not all Greene's similes enhance the narrative. There is an interesting example in the first few pages of *It's a Battlefield*. The Assistant Commissioner has been asked to the meet the minister's private secretary in a restaurant:

He saw the private secretary detach himself from two women. Tall, with round smooth features and ashen hair, he shone with publicity; he had the glamour and consciousness of innumerable photographs. His face was like the plate-glass window of an expensive shop. One could see, very clearly and to the best effect, a few selected objects: a silver casket, a volume of Voltaire exquisitely bound, a self-portrait by an advanced and fashionable Czechoslovakian. (ch. 1)

It is an arresting simile. Shelden has shown that passages from Greene's early novels can be set out in verse to make small imagist poems in the manner of Ezra Pound, and one could do so with this, though the implication of seeing so much in a single face is surrealist rather than imagist. In one sense the simile is brilliantly effective, associating the young man with the expensive high culture of his milieu. Yet to see why it is inappropriate in its context, we need only ask who is seeing him in this way? It is certainly not the Assistant Commissioner, a man with simple tastes and no aesthetic pretensions. Here is an instance of Greene, having had a bright idea, abusing the convention of free indirect style to insert it into the Assistant Commissioner's consciousness. Elsewhere in his writing he is more adroit in relating the human and the inanimate. A few pages further on, as the policeman is being driven through the inner suburbs of south London, Greene presents a simile that is both bold and rich in associations: 'Candahar Road, Khyber Terrace, Kabul Street, the Victorian villas wavered in the mist like a shaking of shakos in old imperial wars'. The exotic names contrast with the drab reality of the district that they adorn, and recall how the Victorian expansion of London, the imperial city, was accompanied by wars in faraway places. And wars are likely to recur in the threatening climate of the present, though the participants will wear steel helmets rather than the picturesque and archaic headgear of earlier wars. Such passages reveal Greene the poet; indeed, the aural effect of 'shaking of shakos' would be more familiar in verse than in prose. His similes and metaphors achieve a particular intensity in some of his early short stories, such as this from 'A Drive in the Country': 'suddenly she saw his love as a mere flicker of gas flame playing on the marshy depth of his irresponsibility.' Or this, an account of the small boy's sense of the odious Mrs Baines in 'The Basement Room': 'she was darkness when the night-light went out in a draught; she was the frozen blocks of earth he had seen one winter in a graveyard when someone said, "They need an electric drill"; she was the flowers gone bad and smelling in the little closet room at Penstanley.'

A poet can content himself with devising and exploring metaphors, but a novelist, even a poetic one, needs to tell a story and invent characters. Greene does so to good effect in *It's a Battlefield*. The Assistant Commissioner, as I have remarked, is a necessary but limited character, serving to focus the author's sense that the world is a battlefield and that so-called primitive life is more authentic than civilization. In his writings about his craft Greene complained that some characters would never come quite alive, while others, intended to be minor figures, do so to an alarming extent and threaten to take over the story, as Minty does in *England Made Me*. The crime reporter Conder plays a busy part in *It's a Battlefield* but he never convinces me of his reality nor of his real necessity to the story. Greene describes him as a fantasist who tries to adopt many roles; the devoted family man 'was only one among the many impersonations of Conder's sad and unsatisfied brain'. We are never told, or shown, why Conder is sad and unsatisfied, and he remains no more than the draft or outline of a complex role-player, with possible affinities with Diderot's character of Rameau's nephew, whom Greene was unable to breathe into life.

The principal female characters, Milly and her sister Kay, are more authentic; Greene presents them both with sympathy if not empathy. Milly is collecting signatures on a petition to reprieve her husband, and there is a good scene when, egged on by the journalist Conder, who sees the potentialities for a story, she visits the widow of the dead policeman. Milly subjects this unfortunate woman, Rose Coney—the first of Greene's fictional Roses—to a good deal of pressure until she finally signs. Kay becomes involved with the wealthy Communist, Mr Surrogate, a widower who claims to be devoted to the memory of his dead wife, but is very ready to take girls to his bed (Greene may have had John Middleton Murry in mind). Surrogate is grotesque but entertaining, a figure out of a Ben Jonson comedy. At the same time Kay is attracted to Jules, a young Anglo-Frenchman who works in a Soho café; their relationship provides the few lyrical moments in the novel.

The most interesting character is, I think, Conrad Drover. He dashes energetically through the story, rather in parallel with the Assistant Commissioner, whom he ends up stalking. Like the policeman, he looks at the world as an outsider. He is something of a type, though that does not stop him being a substantial and disturbing presence. He is a precursor of the Scholarship Boy, who became much discussed in post-war English society, and was quoted as an example by Richard Hoggart in *The Uses of Literacy*. Conrad has moved out of his class by being clever and scrambling up the educational ladder; he is a chief clerk while his brother is a bus driver (though a bus driver in the 1930s would have been part of the aristocracy of labour). But Conrad's career has given him little satisfaction; he remains alienated and insecure:

Brains had only meant that he must work harder in the elementary school and suffer more in the secondary school than those born free of them. At night he could still hear the malicious chorus telling him that he was a favourite of the masters, mocking him for the pretentious name that his parents had fastened on him, like a badge of brains since birth. Brains, like a fierce heat, had turned the world to a desert round him, and across the sands in the occasional mirage he saw the stupid crowds, playing, laughing, and without thought enjoying the tenderness, the compassion, the companionship of love. (ch. 2)

The simile dramatically emphasizes Conrad's apartness from the world, and his unusual Christian name is a particular cause of torment. It provides the occasion for one of Greene's authorial jokes:

His parents had no business calling him by such a name, the name of a sea-man, a merchant officer who once lodged in their house. 'What was there about him?' he had often asked. 'Why call me after him? Was he clever?' 'Not that I know of,' they said. 'Was he kind to you?' 'Not particularly'. 'What happened to him?' 'I dunno. Gave us the idea, I suppose. No good calling you Herbert. Your uncle was broke.' So 'Conrad, Conrad, Conrad' had been flicked at him across the desks, across the asphalt yard, driving him into isolation, while the Jims, the Herberts, the Henrys flocked together and shared secrets. (ch. 4)

(Here the Henrys are used as images of brash normality, which they tend not to be in Greene's later fiction.) Conrad is a dramatic type as well as a sociological one. He is an obsessive, unhappy figure, like the malcontents in Elizabethan and Jacobean drama. His atten-tion is focused on efforts to obtain a reprieve for his brother, though he is haunted by the guilty thought that if Jim is executed he will be able to marry Milly, whom he loves. His mental state is always shaky, and as the novel develops it tips over into madness. He passes the Assistant Commissioner in the street and recognizes who he is, considering him the embodiment of the unjust society that has condemned his brother, and he resolves to kill him. The Commissioner is at first unaware that he is being followed, but before long his professional training makes him conscious of his pursuer though he has no idea of who he is or what he wants. At one point Conrad accosts the Commissioner in the street, and is brushed aide. The policeman assumes he is a beggar, though of respectable appearance, perhaps one of the middle-class victims of economic depression. He then wishes he had done something to help him. The Commissioner has no belief in justice as an abstract concept, though he is aware of the inequalities and deprivation underlying the glitter of metropolitan life. Greene wrote of *It's a*

Battlefield, 'I still think the last sixty pages are as successful as anything I have written since'. He was right. The final section of the novel begins with the brief, tender pastoral adventure of Kay's and Jules's trip into rural Hertfordshire in a hired car. Then comes the compelling account of Conrad's pursuit of the Commissioner through the wet streets of the West End with a revolver in his pocket. It is melodramatic, but it has a Dostoevskyan intensity.

At the end of the novel the Commissioner has survived, and Conrad has not. Jim Drover has been reprieved, but, horrified at the thought of spending the next eighteen years in prison, he unsuccessfully tries to take his life. The prison chaplain who brings this news to the Assistant Commissioner tells him, in distressed tones, that he has had enough of his dispiriting work and is going to resign: 'I can't stand human justice any longer. Its arbitrariness. Its incomprehensibility.' The Commissioner replies that, without wanting to be blasphemous, one could say much the same of divine justice. The chaplain replies, 'Perhaps. But one can't hand in a resignation to God.' He is echoing Ivan Karamazov who, recoiling from human cruelty, resolves to hand his ticket back to God. Greene was a Catholic when he wrote *It's a Battlefield*, but he had not yet embarked on the exploration of religious questions that marked his so-called Catholic novels. However, there is a momentary anticipation of them here.

W. J. West has described *It's a Battlefield* as a political novel. It is true that it presents a panoramic view of metropolitan society and the deep divisions within in it, and it dwells on political questions: class war and the arbitrary nature of human justice. But it is not a political novel in the way that term has been understood by writers on the Left, either in the 1930s or subsequently. Greene regarded himself as a man of the Left and joined the Independent Labour Party. But in this novel the Communists are seen as absurd, and there is no suggestion of the ultimate triumph of progressive forces and the just cause of the workers. Greene's vision may be closer to T. S. Eliot's, who referred in 1923 to 'the immense panorama of futility and anarchy which is contemporary history'. Eliot, who had recently published *The Waste Land*, is discussing *Ulysses*. Both works influenced Greene. The shifting townscapes in *It's a Battlefield* are indebted to Joyce's novel, while the restless succession of sharp images in which Greene evokes contemporary London recalls *The Waste Land*. It was a poem he had long admired and regarded as an example of cinematic collage (the title of his third novel, *Rumour at Nightfall*, alludes to Eliot's poem). *It's a Battlefield* is too much of a melodrama to rise to the heights of tragedy, but it mimes the achievements of Renaissance drama and ends like one. Conrad is dead and Jim is condemned to a living death in a prison cell, and Milly is in a similar condition at home. Elizabethan and Jacobean tragedies tend to soften their bloody blows by leaving young people alive at the end to carry the story on into the future. In *It's a Battlefield* Kay and Jules have ended their rural idyll with an unsatisfactory sexual encounter and the mutual realization that they are not right for each other. But they are young and can still hope. Whatever Greene's own political views when he was writing it, *It's a Battlefield* is a pessimistic novel, which one can see as the work of the Augustinian Christian that Evelyn Waugh a few years later proclaimed Greene to be. It is in evident ways immature and over-ambitious, and too much in Conrad's debt. But its power and poetry make it memorable, though it has been long underrated or ignored. It is, I believe, the best of Greene's pre-war novels after *Brighton Rock*.

After confining himself to London in *It's a Battlefield*, Greene broadened his horizons. Early in 1933 he reviewed a life of the Swedish tycoon and financial criminal Ivar Kreuger, who had achieved a near-monopoly of the match trade and lent large sums of money to governments. But it was all a house of cards and when it collapsed Kreuger committed suicide. Greene found it an absorbing story and resolved to write his next novel about a figure based on Kreuger; in search of material he spent some weeks in Sweden in the summer of 1933, accompanied by his brother Hugh. But he had divided aims: as well as a tale of high finance in a Swedish setting he had more individual and psychological interests. The original title of the novel which became *England Made Me* was *Brother and Sister*. (The novel was reissued in America in 1953 under another rejected title, *The Shipwrecked*.) The principal characters are Anthony and Kate Farrant, a twin brother and sister, thirty-something, in revolt against a conventional bourgeois background and strangely dependent on each other. Anthony is a familiar type: the charming ne'er-do-well, with his plausible manner, his one good suit, his public-school accent, and his impractical schemes for making money; he takes jobs in foreign parts but never holds them down for long and is soon back in England, sponging on his family. Kate is cleverer and more determined. She has in a sense emancipated herself, and has moved to Sweden where she is personal assistant and mistress of the financier Erik Krogh, Greene's version of Kreuger.

In the opening of the novel Kate is in England on a visit and has arranged to meet Anthony in the bar of a railway station; characteristically, he is late:

She might have been waiting for her lover. For three quarters of an hour she had sat on the same high stool, watching the swing door. Behind her the ham sandwiches were piled under a glass dome, the urns gently steamed. As the door swung open, the smoke of engines silted in, grit on the skin and like copper on the tongue. 'Another gin'. It was her third. Damn him, she thought with tenderness, I'm hungry. She swallowed it at a draught, as she was used to drinking schnapps; *skål, skål*, but there was no-one to *skål*. (part I, I)

It is a compelling and evocative opening, which in its attention to visual detail could reasonably be called cinematic. But the information that Kate has been waiting for three-quarters of an hour could not be conveyed in film, which exists in a perpetual present tense, where the passing of time can be conveyed only by such devices as the hands of a clock moving forward or leaves blowing off a calendar. The passage also has literary antecedents. It invokes what Greene later in the novel calls 'the sadness of railway stations', while the first sentence echoes the opening words of a novel that was important to Greene, Henry James's *The Wings of the Dove*: 'She waited, Kate Croy, for her father to come in.' Kate Croy is waiting for her father and Kate Farrant for her brother, though she waits as if he were her lover. Eventually Anthony arrives with an excuse for his lateness that even he does not believe: 'And why, she thought, as she kissed him and touched his back to assure herself that he was there, that he had really come, that they were together, should anyone believe him? He can't open his mouth without lying.' Kate, the stronger character, has always protected him and tried to support him. Once, when they were children, he had run away from his boarding school to meet Kate, and she persuades him to go back to it. Memories of this incident recur in the novel; for Anthony it was a kind of betrayal, bringing in one of Greene's obsessional topics. So, too, were memories of schooldays, as we see from his autobiographical writings. It was a common preoccupation of the Auden generation,* and in 1934 Greene edited *The Old School: Essays by Diverse Hands*.

Kate is devoted to Anthony, even though she sees through him, and the devotion is more than sisterly. In *Ways of Escape* Greene was quite explicit: 'The subject—apart from the economic background of the thirties and that sense of capitalism staggering from crisis to crisis—was simple and unpolitical, a brother and sister in the confusion of incestuous love.' This separation of the personal from

---

* See 'Boys Among Men, Men Among Boys' in my *Reading the Thirties* (London, 1978).

the political indicates divided aims on Greene's part; the different parts of the novel do not cohere well, though its successful aspects are impressive. The transgressive subject of incest—particularly between brother and sister—has always been too sensitive for extensive literary treatment though there are suggestions of it in Gothic novels and Byronic mythology. In an earlier period it was a recurring motif in Jacobean tragedy, as in Ferdinand's guilty passion for his sister in Webster's *The Duchess of Malfi*, a play that Greene greatly admired; in John Ford's *'Tis Pity She's a Whore*, which is late enough to be Caroline rather than Jacobean, the doomed love of the siblings Giovanni and Annabella is central to the tragedy. Greene was well read in the drama of this period—in a film review in 1937 he wrote, by way of praise, 'we are reminded of the Jacobeans at their most bloody and exact'[14]—and I think we can see its influence in *England Made Me* and his other novels of the 1930s. There are places where Greene introduces a Jacobean cadence: Kate is described as watching Anthony with an undisguised devotion, 'a devotion of the blood, not of the brain', a phrase which could occur in Webster or Middleton, and is reminiscent of lines from Cyril Tourneur's *The Atheist's Tragedy*.

> Tush, you mistake the way into a woman.
> The passage lies not through her reason but her blood.

The love of Anthony and Kate is certainly not consummated; it is not even acknowledged by either of them, though Kate comes closer to self-understanding. In *Ways of Escape* Greene refers, rather harshly, to the 'cowardly evasions' of the doomed pair. In fact, neither of them is given the psychological depth and subtlety that could have led to an adequate unfolding of such a difficult theme. By the end of the novel they are indeed doomed but their fate comes from the public world rather than their individual temperaments.

Greene was well aware of what was wrong with the novel, notably the presentation of Krogh and his world, but he was satisfied with the characterization of Anthony and Kate, whom he described as 'the woman I have drawn better than any other, with the possible exception of Sarah in *The End of the Affair*'. One can concede this whilst maintaining that Greene was not very successful with women characters. Kate is individual enough to be neither a waif nor a good-time girl, but her responses to the world are limited, moving between anguish and an unconvincing worldly cynicism. So are Anthony's, but he is more avowedly a type, both in sociological terms and as an example of a Jonsonian humour: 'He had the bold approach, the shallow cheer of an advertisement.' What is most interesting in Greene's portrayal of Anthony—and I think it is successful—is the degree of metaphorical life with which he is invested. In the first few pages the similes have a striking poetic intensity: 'Congratulate me, he seemed to be saying, and his humorous friendly shifty eyes raked her like the headlamps of a second-hand car which had been painted and polished to deceive.' The clashing adjectives define Anthony's character, and the simile opens out to draw in the shabby world in which he lives and moves. The similes dehumanize him by associating him with the mechanical and inanimate. His eyes 'were as blank as the end pages of a book hurriedly turned to hide something too tragic or too questionable on the last leaf'. 'But when he turned his smile explained everything; he carried it always with him as a leper carried his bell; it was a perpetual warning that he was not to be trusted.' Anthony is established as a presence, but by different means from conventional novelistic characterization. Later in the book we read, 'Behind the bright bonhomie of his glance, behind the firm hand-clasp and the easy joke, lay a deep nihilism.' At this point Anthony anticipates the demonic Pinkie of *Brighton Rock*, though *England Made Me* lacks the moral and religious dimensions of the later novel.

The first part of *England Made Me*, set in London, continues the urban poetry of Greene's previous novel: 'Autumn was the few leaves drifted from God knows where upon the pavement by Warren Street tube, the lamplight on the wet asphalt, the gleam of the cheap port in the glasses held by old women in the Ladies' Bar.' But most of the novel is set in Sweden, a country Greene knew only from a fact-finding holiday (years later he came to know it well when he was having an affair with a Swedish actress). He obviously took conscientious notes when he was there and the Swedish settings are shown in plausible detail, though they are inevitably insubstantial when compared with the English ones. The general impression they make I would describe as 'watery'; this is partly because of the presence of canals in Stockholm and its surroundings (one of which becomes of crucial significance at the end of the story), partly because it seems to rain a lot. And beyond this, the descriptions of places suggest the pale charm of a watercolour. Stockholm is Krogh's realm. And Krogh, as Greene was well aware, does not come off; he describes him as one of those characters 'who obstinately refuses to live, who is there only for the sake of the story'. At the same time, he takes up a large part of the action; Kate is his lover and Anthony, at her urging, is appointed to advise him on his clothes and to act as his bodyguard. Originally, one assumes, Greene wanted to write a novel about someone like Ivar Kreuger, and then tried to combine it with his account of sibling love, and the division is evident. The problem with Krogh is not just that he somehow would not come alive, but that Greene simply did not know enough about such a man and the life he would lead; just as the portrait of the Assistant Commissioner in *It's a Battlefield* reflected Greene's ignorance of high-level policing. Krogh is said to be the richest man in Europe, able to affect the fortunes of nations (and, like Kreuger, a crook whose enterprises are sailing very close to the wind). But as Greene describes him he is very much less than a tycoon of the order of Citizen Kane. He has an ultramodern office block as his headquarters, where he is not comfortable, with a prestigious work of avant-garde sculpture in the courtyard which he fails to appreciate. He seems to run his business just with the help of Kate and a few shadowy helpers in the background. He seems vague and sometimes out of his depth, even absurd, hardly a master of the universe. Nevertheless, there are aspects of Krogh that reflect the way the world is going, if only Greene could have plausibly established them. As we would now say, he thinks globally. As Kate puts it, 'But nationality's finished. Krogh doesn't think in frontiers. He's beaten unless he has the world.' In *England Made Me* Greene showed himself very conscious of current advances of modernity: in art and architecture, in popular culture (Greta Garbo, unnamed but unmistakable, is shown as paying a return visit to her native land), and in technology. Aeroplanes play a part in the story; and this must be the first novel anywhere (science fiction apart) that makes a casual passing reference to television, a year or so before the BBC launched the world's first regular service.

If Krogh remains inert, other figures whom Greene intended to be minor come triumphantly alive—as grotesques, not as realistic rounded characters. As Greene put it, 'suddenly the boat listed because Minty came on board'. He describes his genesis:

He was entirely unexpected when he emerged from the pre-conscious—this remittance man who woke up one morning in his Stockholm lodgings watched by a spider under a tooth glass . . . I had required, as a minor figure, some fellow outsider who would recognize—as only a fellow countryman can—the fraudulent element in Anthony, who could detect the falsity of the old Harrovian tie, but I had no intention of introducing into the story a sly pathetic Anglo-Catholic . . . who would steal all the scenes in which he played a part and have the last word, robbing even Kate of her curtain at Anthony's funeral. Oh, yes, I resented Minty, and yet I couldn't keep him down. (*Ways of Escape*, ch. 1, 6)

Minty has lived in Stockholm for many years, receiving a remittance from home and following ill-paid employment as a stringer for a local newspaper and making translations from English into Swedish. He is obsessed with his schooldays at Harrow and his devotions to obscure saints. He hangs around the British Legation and makes determined attempts to get the Minister, another Harrovian, and a minor poet in the manner of Ernest Dowson, to attend the annual Old Boys' dinner. He is casually cruel, keeping a spider under a glass in his room. He realizes that Anthony is not entitled to the Harrovian tie he unwisely wears, but makes needling remarks rather than openly confronting him. At the same time, he is conscious of Anthony's charm. Minty is probably a repressed homosexual of the kind that hates women (perhaps some early scandal in England has led to his exile in Sweden). He lives in poverty and because of the state of his stomach has to let his coffee cool before he can drink it. He has few friends but is maliciously aware of Stockholm gossip. Minty is not a nice man, but like many unpleasant fictional characters he is a fascinating presence. Greene reveals him in a sharp dehumanizing simile: 'He put on his black coat and had trouble with the sleeves; one arm stuck in a torn lining and for a moment he was like a small black splintered pillar set in the open space the room provided.'

Krogh's henchman Fred Hall is another minor character presented with such imaginative power that he threatens to distort the narrative. Once, he and Krogh were young inventors working together on equal terms, but now Krogh is the dominant figure. Hall resents his subservient role but remains totally loyal to his employer, with a strange schoolgirl devotion. He comes across as a quasi-Dickensian figure, with his flat narrow skull, his tight brown overcoat, his brown hat with a turned-up brim, his watch chain, his cockney accent. But he is what would nowadays be called a hard man, with a short fuse and a taste for violence, who always carries knuckledusters in his pocket; at one point he is described as 'the thin furious figure'. He is smart enough to act as Krogh's financial agent in Amsterdam whilst being willing to get his hands dirty in his master's service. He knows the world, is widely travelled, and has a limited but adequate command of languages. He is, in Jacobean terms, Krogh's 'instrument', 'a wondrous necessary man', like Middleton's De Flores. Krogh speaks to Hall by telephone and tells him that he needs him back in Sweden urgently. Hall flies from Amsterdam to Malmö by a Dutch passenger plane called the Scandinavian Air Express; Greene's description of the flight gives a wonderfully vivid account of the early days of commercial air travel. Hall provides an early instance of bad behaviour in the air by retreating to the lavatory to smoke an illicit cigarette: 'He swung his legs and spat out small perfect rings, endangering the lives of twelve passengers, a pilot, a wireless operator, and several thousand pounds of property. A little thing like that did not worry Fred Hall.' Greene intervenes in Hall's consciousness to provide an imagistic evocation of the airports of Europe at that time, as he had seen or imagined them:

He knew the airports of Europe as well as he had once known the stations of the Brighton line; shabby Le Bourget; the great scarlet rectangle of the Tempelhof as one came in from London in the dark, the headlamp lighting up the asphalt way; the white sand blowing up round the shed at Talinn; Riga, where the Berlin to Leningrad plane came down and bright pink mineral waters were sold in a tin-roofed shed; the huge aerodrome at Moscow with machines parked half a dozen deep, the pilots taxi-ing casually here and there, trying to find room, bouncing back and forth, beckoned by one official with his cap askew. (part 5, 3)

This presents an early twentieth-century equivalent to the nineteenth-century romanticism about railway stations.

Hall meets Krogh when he is dining in a hotel, and does some instant dirty work for him by seeing off a young Swede, one of his

employees who has tracked the tycoon to protest against his
father's sacking. When he refuses to leave, Hall briskly and brutally
beats him up while the restaurant orchestra plays one of Greene's
invented pop songs, in a sharp example of the Flaubertian super-
imposition of narratives.

> I'm waiting, dear,
> Leave off hating, dear,
> Let's talk of mating, dear,
> I'm lonely.

An odd subsidiary strand in the narrative concerns Professor
Hammarsten, an eccentric academic who teaches English literature
and moonlights as a journalist. He has translated Shakespeare's
Pericles and wants to put on a production of his version, which he
persuades Krogh to finance. This episode permits Greene to engage
his grim sense of humour at Hammarsten's expense; he is a fool
who does not realize that Gower, who speaks the prologue, was a
medieval poet. *Pericles* is chronologically a Jacobean play, though a
romance rather than a tragedy, and in the prologue, which
Hammarsten recites, there is a reference to the guilty but fashionable motif of incest. In the events preceding the action of the play
King Antiochus has misbehaved with his daughter:

> With whom the father liking took,
> And her to incest did provoke.

(I have sometimes wondered if Greene's mocking portrayal of this
Swedish scholar was one of the reasons why he was refused the
Nobel Prize for Literature.) As the novel draws towards its conclusion, Greene seems if anything over-anxious to emphasize the topic
of incest. A blonde Swedish girl whom Anthony has picked up in
a restaurant, and who speaks 'with Garbo in her voice', sees Kate
and asks, 'Is that your sister?' Anthony says it is, and she responds,

'I don't believe you. You're in love with her.' In her final scene with Anthony Kate remembers how as children they could communicate telepathically with each other, and she says she still knows what he is thinking. There is a brief, perverse exchange:

'But I do love you, Kate. Honestly'.
'Like that. In that tone. This is how I love you, Anthony'. She drove at his fingers with her penknife. He whipped them away.
'For Heaven's sake, Kate…'
'The lover's pinch, Tony, which hurts and—'
'You nearly cut me'.
'Poor Tony, give it here. I'll make it well.'

Kate quotes from *Anthony and Cleopatra*—'The stroke of death is as a lover's pinch, | Which hurts, and is desired'—but the feeling is momentarily closer to Ford's *'Tis Pity*. In *Ways of Escape* Greene finds fault with Kate and Anthony for not fully facing and accepting their feelings; but the ultimate fault is the author's for introducing a theme which was too intense and problematical for him to handle adequately, and for awkwardly linking with it an exposure of international finance.

At the end of the novel Anthony has succumbed to the high mortality rate which afflicts Greene's central characters. There is a cremation—the first of several in Greene's novels—which is regarded with great distaste by the Anglo-Catholic Minty, who has come to report on the ceremony. As such occasions do, it brings together the surviving characters: Krogh, Kate, Hammarsten, Hall. Minty learns that Krogh's enterprise, which he knew had been on the edge of disaster, has been saved by a new share issue. Kate was going to enter a loveless marriage with Krogh, but has now left him and his employment and is about to take up a job in Copenhagen; she reverts to her cynical vein, ' "We're all thieves," Kate said. "Stealing a livelihood here and there, giving nothing back." ' In the air above Stockholm, Krogh and the modern world are having the last word: 'rising and falling like a flight of swallows, the sun catch-ing their aluminium wings as they turned, came the aeroplanes, a dozen at least, making the sky noisy with their engines as the sound of the organ died away.' In the early decades of the twentieth century the aeroplane was a symbol of power and freedom, celebrated by the Italian Futurists and the English poets of the Auden genera-tion (though by the 1930s the aesthetic potentiality of the aeroplane was threatened by its sinister role as a bomber). But these circling aeroplanes are not there for the bird-like beauty of their flight: as they fly they begin skywriting 'Krogh' in the sky over the city.*

I have remarked on the Jacobean traces in *England Made Me*. A few years after that novel Greene wrote *British Dramatists*, a short illustrated study that was part of a wartime series illustrating the achievements of British culture. In that book he observes of the Jacobeans:

Of all these dramatists Webster stands alone by virtue of his one great play, *The Duchess of Malfi*, the only play of which it is possible to say that, owing nothing to Shakespeare, it yet stands on a level with the great tragedies. *The White Devil* had showed him to be a poet of some erratic genius: it would have left a memory of morbid and magnificent lines: we should have remembered him with Ford and Tourneur, a group who shared a kind of dark horror, a violent moral anarchy which seems to have followed the Elizabethan age like a headache after a feast. Among these writers you are aware of no moral centre, no standard of moral criticism—your hero may be an incestuous murderer, the most moving lines may be put in the mouth of an adultress who has plotted the murder of her husband. In *King Lear* the cruelty of the world may appal us, but somewhere outside there is virtue: the seventeenth century is not eternity, and death is an escape and not an end. But in Tourneur and the earlier Webster we are in the company of men who would really seem to have been lost in the dark night of the soul if they had had enough religious sense to feel despair: the world is all there is, and the world is violent, mad, miserable and without point.[15]

---

* See 'The Last Days of Futurism' in my *Reading the Thirties* (London, 1978).

Greene seems to identify with the sombre vision of the Jacobeans, but still has enough religious sense to see beyond it. His account is, I think, relevant to *England Made Me*, which presents a bleak world of power and betrayal, deceit and violence. I find the novel is most rewarding when it is read as a poetic drama rather than a novel in the realistic tradition. It contains the flickering, intermittently intense poetry of the Jacobeans; the guilty concern with incest; and memorable figures who are types or grotesques. Read in this way it is easier to accept its artistic flaws, particularly the division between the public world of Krogh and the private one of Kate and Anthony. What would be unacceptable in a carefully planned novel is likely to get by in the looser scheme of the drama. Even so great a play as *The Duchess of Malfi* goes to pieces after the death of the Duchess, a whole act before it ends. There is a relevant remark in the Allott and Ferris study on the presence of Greene's obsessions: 'Greene's novels from *It's a Battlefield* onwards belong to the type of poetic novel in which the obsessions are close to the surface: in them structure is used emphatically, alongside character and situation to project the total poetic meaning.'[16]

NOTES

1. Shelden, *Graham Greene* (London, 1994), 97.

2. Greene, *The Pleasure Dome* (London, 1972), 133–4.

3. K. W. Gransden, 'Graham Greene's Rhetoric', *Essays in Criticism*, 31 (1981), 41–60.

4. David Lodge, *The Novelist at the Crossroads* (London, 1971), 94

5. Shelden, *Greene*, 97.

6. Lodge, *Novelist at the Crossroads*, 94.

7. Sergei Eisenstein, *Film Form*, trans. and ed. Jay Leda (London, 1963), 154.

8. In David Lodge, *Working with Structuralism* (London, 1981).

9. Graham Greene, *In Search of a Character* (London, 1961), 9.

10. Greene, *The Pleasure Dome*, 10.

11. *Film Form*, 12.

12. Greene, *The Pleasure Dome*, 12.
13. M.-F. Allain, *The Other Man* (Harmondsworth, 1984), 130–1.
14. Greene, *The Pleasure Dome*, 142.
15. Greene, *British Dramatists* (London, 1942), 15.
16. K. Allott and M. Ferris, *The Art of Graham Greene* (London, 1951), 15.

ADDITIONAL NOTES (2008)

p. 40 My claim that there was never a part of the London Underground called the 'Outer Circle' has been challenged. It is true that, as Christian Wolmar points out in his authoritative book *The Subterranean Railway*, for some years at the end of the nineteenth century there was a service called the 'Outer Circle' that ran on the tracks of the District Line and the North London Railway. But it was never a line in its own right, and I remain convinced that Greene deliberately changed the 'Inner Circle' (now the Circle Line) into the 'Outer Circle' to sustain a parallel with Dante.

p. 48 In a 'Fiction Chronicle' published in 1936 Greene discusses the importance of the opening sentence in a novel: 'An artist is unlikely to show his purpose with more conviction and concentration than in the moment when he first puts pen to paper'. He quotes the opening sentence of *The Wings of the Dove* as exemplifying 'the intense moral passion' of James's novel. Ian Thomson, ed., *Articles of Faith: the Collected Tablet' Journalism of Graham Greene* (Oxford, 2006), 86

3

Entertainments

SOME time after it was published Greene decided that later editions of *Stamboul Train* would describe it as an 'entertainment'. Then in 1936 he published *A Gun for Sale*, a novel that was specifically called 'an entertainment' on the title page, establishing a sub-genre of his own fiction. Eventually, when he was preparing the Collected Edition, Greene abandoned the distinction. The entertainments that he wrote in the late 1930s and 1940s were, indeed, not all that different from the books he regarded as novels, but they drew more directly on the conventions of popular fiction and allowed Greene to indulge his liking for melodrama. They were also very conscious of threatening historical forces. *A Gun for Sale* is a gripping thriller though of a very literary kind, full of quotations from, or allusions to, poems and plays. It opens with a murder and turns into a manhunt, with armed police in pursuit of an armed fugitive. Most of the novel takes place in darkness or fog. I have remarked on scenes that seem indebted to contemporary French films; the presentation of violent action also suggests American crime movies and anticipates the *film noir* of the 1940s. The opening scene, describing the murder of a Central European statesman by a hired contract-killer, is the most powerful in the book. Its sharp attention to visual detail invites the description 'cinematic', but that is so only in the way in which it is true of Mr Verloc's murder in *The Secret Agent*. After shooting the minister the killer shoots his elderly female secretary as she tries to escape. These events are shown through the killer's consciousness, but Greene employs free indirect style to make authorial interventions, as when we read, 'who would have imagined an old woman could be so tough?' This is a parodic echo of Lady Macbeth's question in Act V of Shakespeare's proto-Jacobean tragedy: 'Yet who would have thought the old man to have had so much blood in him?' If one aspect of *A Gun for Sale* shows Greene's desire to write a contemporary thriller, another shows how his imagination was still caught by the violence and intrigue of Elizabethan and Jacobean drama. The killer, James Raven, is initially presented as an affectless automaton as he carries out the murder. But later in the narrative he shows violent feeling, seeing himself as a victim of society. He has reasons for this. His father was hanged for murder and his mother committed suicide by cutting her throat. The orphaned boy was brought up in an 'industrial school' and he has turned to crime in adult life. His bitterness is increased by a disfiguring hare-lip which was not properly treated in childhood. Raven is a forceful creation, but in the manner of English Renaissance drama not of the realistic novel. He has Shakespearian antecedents: Richard III in his sense of a distinguishing deformity, and Thersites in his railing against life. But he is closer to the desperate men of the Jacobeans, who have lost any moral sense they may have had, though they crave recognition, and will do anything for money: Flamineo, Bosola, De Flores. At one point Raven remarks, 'There's hell coming to somebody for this', a sentiment they would have understood. When he returns to England after the murder he is paid for his work. But he has been double-crossed by his employers; the money has been stolen, it is in £5 notes, a conspicuously large denomination at that time, and the numbers have been circulated by the police. When Raven tries to spend one of these notes it is identified and he has to make a sudden retreat. Henceforth he is on the run, suspected of robbery, not of murder. He has plenty of money which he cannot spend, and his hare-lip makes him easily identified. But he is determined both to evade pursuit and to revenge himself on his employers. At the end he succeeds: he kills his betrayers, and is himself shot by the police; in Jacobean style, the stage is littered with corpses. Raven is an early and inchoate version of Pinkie in *Brighton Rock*, and Greene risks sentimentality in trying to humanize him after his initial portrayal of him as totally ruthless.

Even within the conventions of the thriller, *A Gun for Sale* strains plausibility: there is an excess of coincidence and many trailing loose ends. The initial murder has been set up by an ageing armaments tycoon, known only as 'Sir Marcus', who wants to start a European war in order to increase business. For much of the narrative his plan seems to be succeeding, and in the background an increasing threat of war is counterpointed with preparations for Christmas. Raven, on the run, with no money that he can safely spend, seems to go for several days without eating, drinking, or sleeping. He has a gun, and when he uses it the police start firing back, in the manner of American rather than English policemen. Yet despite weaknesses in the plot, the novel presents interesting imaginative life of a rather bizarre kind. There are only two 'normal' people. The stolid Scotland Yard detective, Jim Mather, is a younger version of the Assistant Commissioner in *It's a Battlefield*: 'he liked to feel that he was one of thousands more or less equal working for a concrete end—not equality of opportunity, not government by the people or by the richest or the best, but simply to do away with crime which meant uncertainty.' Jim is engaged to Anne Crowder, who thinks of him as 'comforting like a large dog'. Anne is a chorus girl, like Coral in *Stamboul Train*, and is one of Greene's resourceful waifs.

The action moves to the Midland city of Nottwich, based on Nottingham, where Greene had spent some months as a trainee journalist. Anne goes there to appear in a pantomime. Raven is in pursuit of Sir Marcus, whose firm, Midland Steel, is based there. When Raven is reported to be in the city Jim Mather, who is on his case, arrives to investigate. Meanwhile Raven has abducted Anne, treating her as protective cover; at first she tries to resist but then, on hearing his sad story (and not knowing he is a murderer), feels sorry for him and stays with him voluntarily. Anne, one feels, is too good-natured to live, but she survives.

Apart from Jim and Anne, all the characters are grotesques, caricatures, and humours. Raven is an obvious instance, while Cholmondeley (otherwise Davis) would fit into a Ben Jonson comedy. He is very fat, he wears an emerald ring, has an insatiable appetite for ice cream and chocolates, and lecherously pursues chorus girls. He is in complete contrast to Sir Marcus, who is ancient and frail and lives on dry biscuits and warm milk. Raven gets them both in the end. Early in the novel, there is Alice, the hunch-backed girl whom Raven is fond of and for whom he buys a dress (fatally, with one of the stolen notes), only to have her spurn him with contempt, increasing his bitterness. He calls on Dr Yogel, a shady medical man with 'a plump hard bonhomous face, a thick sensual mouth'. Raven has heard of him as someone with a sideline as an abortionist, and wants to know if Yogel can do anything to correct his hare-lip, but without success.

Nottwich provides some remarkable characters, notably Acky and Tiny, a rather mad elderly couple who show the extent to which minor figures, who appear only for a few pages, can acquire an unexpected life and solidity. Acky is an unfrocked clergyman who spends his time composing a letter of complaint to his bishop; when crossed he produces a string of Latin obscenities. Their role in the plot is to provide a room for Mr Cholmondeley's assignations. The Chief Constable is a pompous clown, henpecked by his wife and a bully to his subordinates, who dreams lovingly of his spell of military service—in a safe and lowly administrative post—during the First World War. Sir Marcus appears for only a few pages, but makes a strong impression as a malign and sinister presence. In one of the occasional powerfully poetic passages in the novel he is described in an image which might have appealed to Webster or Donne, those writers much possessed by death: 'Sir Marcus was as painfully aware of his bones as a skeleton must be, wearing itself away against the leaden lining of its last suit.' Among the lesser characters is Buddy Fergusson, a crass, burly, and inept medical student, who comes across as another Jonsonian type, energetically drawn. For all its violent story there is a recurring note of grim farce in *A Gun for Sale*, a characteristically Jacobean combination. Cholmondeley is attempting, very clumsily, to seduce Anne when he realizes that she is in league with Raven, who is lurking in the street outside. In some way—we are not told how—he overpowers her, ties her up, and shoves her up the chimney. Later she is rescued by Raven, none the worse for wear though a little shaken, and still indomitably cheerful. This bizarre and incredible episode belongs to folklore rather than to the thriller, no matter how stylized. One has, I think, to see it as one of Greene's jokes, perhaps a reference to Cholmondeley's frustrated desire.

Later in the novel there is a mock air raid on Nottwich as part of a civil defence exercise. Since gas attacks were a potential danger, gas masks had to be worn by anyone in the street. They give people a grotesque appearance and also make an effective disguise, as Raven realizes. He steals Buddy Fergusson's gas mask and medical student's white coat and thus disguised makes his way into Midland Steel to carry out the final murders. He kills Sir Marcus and Cholmondeley and aims at Jim Mather, who is dangling perilously outside the window on a painter's platform:

Raven watched him with bemused eyes, trying to take aim. It wasn't a difficult shot, but it was almost as if he had lost interest in killing. He was only
aware of a pain and despair which was more like a complete weariness
than anything else. He couldn't work up any sourness, any bitterness, at
his betrayal . . . he had been marked from his birth for this end, to be
betrayed in turn by everyone until every avenue into life was safely closed:
by his mother bleeding in the basement, by the chaplain at the home, by
the shady doctor off Charlotte Street. How could he have expected to
escape the commonest betrayal of all: to go soft on a skirt? . . . For the first
time the idea of his mother's suicide came to him without bitterness, as he
reluctantly fixed his aim and Saunders shot him in the back through the
opening door. Death came to him in the form of unbearable pain. It was as
if he had to deliver this pain as a woman delivers a child, and he sobbed and
moaned in the effort. At last it came out of him and he followed his only
child into a vast desolation.

This is both melodramatic and poetic; at this point, in an uneven
narrative of mixed generic modes, some of Greene's deepest
obsessions are given eloquent expression: the inevitability of
betrayal (Raven believes that Anne has betrayed him) and the
possibility of suicide, which was to prove irresistible to Scobie in
The Heart of the Matter and Rose Pemberton in *The Living Room*,
among others. (We learn in passing that Jim Mather's brother has
killed himself.)

A Gun for Sale is composed of several interwoven strands derived
from Greene's own obsessions, from Jacobean drama, and from
contemporary thrillers and crime films. History, national and international, provides another strand. As I have remarked, Greene was
very interested in the changes in English society in the 1930s even
when he did not like them. There is a good example in the new
housing estate on the edge of Nottwich, where Raven takes refuge
in an unoccupied house in 'Shakespeare Avenue', which is so jerry-
built that a lock can be forced with very little effort. Louis MacNeice

noted such estates in his poem 'Birmingham':

Splayed outwards through the suburbs houses, houses for rest
Seducingly rigged by the builder, half-timbered houses with lips pressed
So tightly and eyes staring at the traffic through bleary haws
And only a six-inch grip of the racing earth in their concrete claws . . .

Such developments, however tawdry, pointed towards further changes
in society. As the 1930s went on, they were increasingly threatened
by the possibility of war, a fear which dominates *A Gun for Sale*. By
1936, when Greene's novel appeared, it was becoming general. In
that year the spectacular Wells–Korda film *Things to Come* showed
the bombing of London, four years before it happened in reality. In
England Made Me aeroplanes are featured for their commercial possibilities: rapid travel and advertising. In *A Gun for Sale* the emphasis
is on their warlike uses, as bombers fly overhead during the civil
defence exercise. The anti-gas precautions reflected the assumption
that gas would be used in air raids. It was this belief that led to the
general distribution of gas masks by the government at the start of
the Second World War, though gas was never used by either side,
probably for fear of reprisals. In the novel, movements towards war,
following the armament manufacturers' diabolical plan, loom
menacingly in the background, and the narrative is shot through
with images and memories of the First World War. Like other
prominent writers of the Auden generation, Greene was old enough
to have been very conscious of the conflict that had claimed fathers
and elder brothers, though too young to take part in it himself.
The assumption that the murder of a prominent statesman
would be sufficient to trigger a war is based in the assassination
of the Archduke Franz Ferdinand in 1914. Major Calkin, the Chief
Constable, 'remembered for some reason the war, the tribunal, the
fun it had all been giving hell to the conchies'. He still has his army
uniform and hopes to wear it again if there is a new war. The absurd

Buddy Fergusson fantasizes about himself as 'the daredevil of the trenches'. In contrast, a hotel doorman has been a real soldier, who wears the Mons medal and the Military Medal on his uniform and has been three times wounded. Allusions to Rupert Brooke's '1914' sequence are embedded in the text: 'a corner of a foreign field' (which Major Calkin thinks is by Shakespeare), 'swimmers into cleanness leaping'.

After the bloody removal of the principal actors the threat of war is lifted, since the *casus belli* is revealed in the nick of time to have been a crime and not a political act. The original conspiracy had been implausible, although such schemes were widely believed in at the time; in fact, though arms manufacturers might have been opportunistically happy to exploit an existing conflict (as they still do), they would have been unlikely to promote a war in which their assets were liable to destruction from the air. If the war is implausible, its sudden calling off at the last minute is equally so; once war fever has been aroused, it is not so easily abated. But, as we are often reminded, despite the obsessive realism of observation in the novel, it is not a peace of realistic writing. An element of romance pervades the conclusion when Jim and Anne return to London, which is evoked with touches of urban poetry: 'the train drew into London over a great viaduct under which the small bright shabby streets ran off like the rays of a star with their sweet shops, their Methodist chapels, their messages chalked on the paving stones'. Anne has the final word: ' "Oh," she said with a sigh of unshadowed happiness, "we're home".' And so they are, with a few years ahead of them before the bombs fall.

A Gun for Sale was followed in 1938 by *Brighton Rock*, which Greene originally intended to be an entertainment, until his realization of the book's depths and implications caused him to take it out of that category; I defer discussion of it until the following chapter. His next entertainment was *The Confidential Agent*, published just before the outbreak of the Second World War in 1939. He wrote of it, 'The Spanish Civil War furnished the background, but it was the Munich Agreement which provided the urgency.' At that time, in September 1938, the war which had been foreshadowed in *A Gun for Sale* seemed about to start, though at the last minute it was put off for a year. The composition of *The Confidential Agent* represented an extraordinary feat of forced labour on Greene's part. He wanted to start work on *The Power and the Glory*, the deeply serious novel that distilled the experiences of his recent visit to Mexico. But he knew it was not likely to sell widely, and the need to provide for his family made him decide to embark on a saleable quasi-thriller, and to write both books simultaneously. He rented a room in Mecklenburg Square—later destroyed by bombs—and worked in the mornings on *The Confidential Agent*, which he completed in six weeks, and then in a more leisurely way on *The Power and the Glory* in the afternoons. It is remarkable that despite this killing pressure of work neither book seems hurried or fatigued in the writing. But, Greene remarked, 'Six weeks of a benzedrine breakfast diet left my nerves in shreds and my wife suffered the result.'

The Confidential Agent brings Greene's archetypal theme of the hunted man into the historical context of a war that is going on in one part of Europe and threatening the rest of it. A fast-moving political thriller, clearly indebted to Buchan, it is closer to actual contemporary politics than *It's a Battlefield* and more historically located than *A Gun for Sale*. The central character 'D.' is the confidential agent who has come to England from a country divided by civil war, to order coal for his government. Greene never mentions Spain, but it is evident that the government in question is that of Republican Spain, while his opponent 'L.' is an agent of the Nationalist side, engaged on the same mission. D. was a distinguished scholar in peacetime and is now a government agent. His wife has been killed in an air raid and he himself was buried

under rubble. Greene wrote, 'D., the chivalrous agent and professor of Romance literature, is not really one of my characters'. In
fact he is an early version of the solitary, alienated, and depressed
figures who move through Greene's novels from the 1950s onwards.
At the same time, he has some affinities with the Assistant
Commissioner of *It's a Battlefield*, in his belief in sticking to a job
without taking a moral line.

The Confidential Agent is technically interesting and innovatory.
Before it, Greene's novels had been narrated from multiple points of
view; and when the narrative was confined to a particular character's
consciousness the author preserved the liberty to move in and out of
it in free indirect style. In *The Confidential Agent*, though the story is
told in the third person, most of it is filtered through D.'s thoughts
and perceptions; they have, one might add, a very Greeneish tinge:
'He had imagined that the suspicion which was the atmosphere of his
own life was due to civil war, but he began to believe that it existed
everywhere: it was part of human life. People were united by their
vices; there was honour among adulterers and thieves.' Since D. is a
highly educated and intelligent man, the author does not have to face
the challenge of presenting the action through a limited consciousness. D. has been to London before and he speaks English well; he
observes the city still at peace with increasing incredulity.

Soon after he arrives in England D. realizes that the other side are
after him, under the leadership of L., an urbane but determined
aristocrat, who is something of a grotesque figure: 'thin as celery
inside his thick coat, tall, he had an appearance of nerves and
agility; he walked fast on legs like stilts, stiffly, but you felt they
might fold up.' L. stands for power and privilege; D., though
unpolitical by temperament, has aligned himself with the poor
and deprived. This was the conventional left-liberal view of the
Spanish Civil War, though for a Catholic like Greene it was complicated by the anti-religious persecution, the murder of priests and

destruction of churches, that was a feature of Republican Spain. He had sided with the Catholic Basques, who were fighting their own private war against the centralizing force of General Franco, and he had intended to visit their territory, but the Basques were defeated before he could arrive.

D.'s principal ally is the Honourable Rose Cullen, whom he runs into at Dover after he arrives and who gives him a lift to London in a hired car when he has missed his train. She, as it happens (coincidences occur thickly in this entertainment), is the daughter of Lord Benditch, the industrialist and mine-owner from whom D. wants to order coal. Rose has radical sympathies, and is a new female type for Greene, neither a plucky waif nor a good-time girl. If anything, she is an icon from the popular songs of the thirties, like Duke Ellington's 'Sophisticated Lady' or Noël Coward's 'Poor Little Rich Girl'. On the way to London Rose and D. stop for dinner at a roadhouse, where D. has a brutal encounter with a Nationalist agent. During dinner they listen to a song—one of Greene's adroit inventions—from a cabaret artist:

People set down their wine and listened as if it were poetry. Even the girl stopped eating for a while. The self-pity of it irritated him; it was a vice nobody in his country on either side the line had an opportunity of indulging.

> 'I don't say you lie: it's just the modern way.
> I don't intend to die: in the old Victorian way.'

He supposed it represented the 'spirit of the age', whatever that meant; he almost preferred the prison cell, the law of flight, the bombed house, his enemy by the door. He watched the girl moodily; there was a time in his life when he would have tried to write her a poem—it would have been better than this.

> 'It was just day-dreaming—I began to discern it:
> It was just a way of talking—and I've started to learn it.'

She said, 'It's muck isn't it? But it has a sort of appeal.' (part 1, 1)

The episode is an example of the Flaubertian juxtaposition of clashing modes of reality; and the same thing could be said of the whole novel, in which D.'s experience of war is brought into continual contrast with the innocence of an England still, though not for much longer, at peace. (*The Confidential Agent* is one of those literary works that reflect the state of consciousness on the eve of the Second World War, such as George Orwell's *Coming up for Air*, Louis MacNeice's *Autumn Journal*, and Virginia Woolf's *Between the Acts*.) There is a powerful statement of the contrast later in the novel, where Greene, having momentarily taken over the narrative from D., provides one of his panoramic views of London:

But D. had no more to say, as they bumped slowly on across the Park. The soap-box orators talked in the bitter cold at Marble Arch with their mackintoshes turned up against their Adam's apples, and all down the road the cad cars waited for the right easy girls, and the cheap prostitutes sat hopelessly in the shadows, and the blackmailers kept an eye open on the grass where the deeds of darkness were quietly and unsatisfactorily accomplished. This was technically known as a city at peace. A poster said: 'Bloomsbury Tragedy Sensation'. (part, 2, 2)

'Deed of darkness' occurs in Shakespeare's *Pericles* (4, vi), but Greene may also be recalling a passage in Act V of *King Lear*, in which Edgar says he has been 'a serving man, proud in heart of mind, that curled my hair, wore gloves in my cap, cap, served the lust of my mistress' heart and did the act of darkness with her.' (Thirty years later Greene used the phrase 'act of darkness' in *Travels with My Aunt*.) Greene's feelings about sexuality seem to have become increasingly gloomy as the threat of war increased.

Soon after they meet, Rose tells D. that she cannot stand melodrama. But Greene regarded melodrama as one of the constituent elements of his art, and despite herself she is caught up in it as she decides to help him in his mission. The plot is superficially complex, not always completely intelligible, and develops rapidly. There are elements of Greene's grim humour, and D. encounters a variety of grotesques and eccentrics. He finds that the contacts who are supposed to help him are really traitors, even in his country's embassy, but Rose proves dependable. He eludes his pursuers and travels to the mining area in the north Midlands from which the vital coal is to come. His mission has been betrayed and failed, but he is determined to prevent the other side from getting the coal. And in this, after some lively melodramatic developments, he is successful: both sides are defeated.

On an initial reading *The Confidential Agent* works as a thriller, but its most interesting and memorable aspects transcend the plot. The metropolitan setting in the first part of the novel is well realized, with scenes in a shabby private hotel in Bloomsbury, a shady language school overlooking Oxford Street, a West End super cinema where D. takes refuge from his pursuers, noticing how much more opulent such places have become since he was last in London. He is baffled when he notices crowds of people cheering two small girls being transported in a Daimler; he learns that they are two princesses (one of whom is the present Queen). The presentation of London conveys Greene's farewell to a city at peace. D.'s trip to the north Midlands provides an opportunity for a different kind of descriptive writing. He has to change trains before dawn at a small halt in a dreary area that is partly rural, partly industrial. The account of daybreak and D.'s gradual perception of the scene is a masterly piece of descriptive prose, and though a gratuitous insertion into the thriller it shows that Greene's literary power was unaffected by the punishing pace at which *The Confidential Agent* was written. The mining area represents a world that was passing; in fact, the mines have been closed because of the industrial depression, and the Spanish contract provides a hope of reopening them. Greene also shows his curiosity about the new manifestations of culture and society in the 1930s. D. has been helped in his flight by Rose, who has influential friends, and he is installed in a smart new hotel on the south coast. It is a very new kind of hotel, designed like an ocean liner and offering all kinds of recreational amenities: Greene later remarked that he had anticipated one of the characteristic manifestations of post-war England, the holiday camp. It is worth remarking that though Greeneland is now considered, almost by definition, to involve exotic settings, in his earlier career Greene saw himself as essentially a novelist of English life. In 1938 he told Julian Maclaren-Ross, 'I try to restrict myself to home ground if I can, English backgrounds, London wherever possible.' Greene acknowledged he had sometimes broken this rule, but added, 'all the same, I think an English writer should write about England.'[1] History was to change all that.

With *The Confidential Agent* Greene bade farewell to pre-war England, as D. does in its closing pages. He has been smuggled on to a small coaster waiting in the Channel, bound for Republican Spain, and finds that Rose is on board waiting for him. He has failed in his mission and has no reason to expect his beleaguered government to be merciful to him. And when the Republic is defeated the Nationalists will certainly not be. Rose is in love with him and wants to stay with him as long as he is alive. The final words are measured and full of implication, with a faint echo of Tennyson's 'Crossing the Bar': 'The light went by astern: ahead there was only the splash, the long withdrawal, and the dark. She said, "you'll be dead very soon: you needn't tell me that, but *now…*" '

In Greene's next entertainment, *The Ministry of Fear*, the war that threatened in *A Gun for Sale* and *The Confidential Agent* is happening all around, and the bombs that were anticipated in air-raid rehearsals, or reported from foreign wars, are falling on

London. Like two other novels published in the same year, Henry Green's *Caught* and James Hanley's *No Directions, The Ministry of Fear* evokes the Blitz on London. It was written in 1942 when Greene was working as an intelligence agent in West Africa, and it made use of the experiences that he described in his journal, 'London 1940–1941', included in *Ways of Escape*. He wrote that on the voyage to Africa he was seized by the idea of writing 'a funny and fantastic thriller'. As I have remarked, Greene had a sense of humour, of an odd kind, and the plot he had devised struck him as funny:

a man acquitted of the murder of his wife by a jury (though he knows his own guilt) who finds himself pursued for a murder of which he was entirely innocent but which he believes he has committed. It sounds a bit complicated told like that, and long before I finished the book I realized the story was not after all very funny, though it might have other merits. (*Ways of Escape*, ch. 4, 1)

The Ministry of Fear is, indeed, not very funny, though it is 'fantastic' to the point of phantasmagoria; 'a bit complicated' absurdly understates the case. The central figure of the story, Arthur Rowe, was acquitted of the mercy-killing of his sick wife on the grounds of temporary madness, was institutionalized for a time and then released. At the start of the narrative he is a solitary with a small private income, cut off from the world—his mental instability apparently stops him taking regular employment—who lives alone in a room in Bloomsbury, where he continually rereads *The Old Curiosity Shop* and *David Copperfield*. In his appearance he seems to owe something to Greene himself, and like D. in *The Confidential Agent* is perhaps an early draft of what I call the 'Greene Man' of the later novels: 'He was a tall stooping lean man with black hair going grey and a sharp narrow face, nose a little twisted out of the straight and a too sensitive mouth.' Greene usually started his novels well, and the opening of *The Ministry of Fear* is both vivid and thematically significant:

There was something about a fête which drew Arthur Rowe irresistibly, bound him like a helpless victim to the distant blare of a band and the knock-knock of wooden balls against coconuts. Of course this year there were no coconuts because there was a war on: you could tell that too from the untidy gaps between the Bloomsbury houses—a flat fireplace half-way up a wall, like the painted fireplace in a cheap dolls' house, and lots of mirrors and green wall-papers, and from round a corner of the sunny afternoon the sound of glass being swept up, like the lazy noise of the sea on a shingled beach. (ch. 1,1)

The description blends the destruction of war with images of peace: the vanished coconut-shies, and the sound of the sea on a beach. Arthur Rowe lives in the past, with his memories and his guilt, in the world that vanished on 31 of August 1939. Most of the story is told through his consciousness and it is an unreliable consciousness. These factors contribute to the phantasmagoric atmosphere (enhanced by the fog which, as in Greene's previous entertainments, swirls freely about). In the opening paragraphs the repeated word 'fête' suggests its homophone 'fate', and is shortly reinforced by 'fortune': 'The fête called him like innocence'. Rowe goes to a fortune-teller at the fête, but she is expecting someone else, and from this confusion many troubles unfold. The general dislocation is enacted in Greene's narrative. In his novels of the 1930s there had been frequent descriptions of London, showing his informed knowledge of the city and his capacity to make a panoramic presentation. Now there are no coherent perspectives. Sheltering in the Tube, Rowe reflects, 'I'm hiding underground, and up above the Germans are methodically smashing London to bits all round me.' But amidst the destruction Greene is still the acute observer, with a startling power of metaphor: 'In Gower Street they were sweeping up glass, and a building smoked into the new day like a candle which some late reveller had forgotten to snuff.' Another arresting simile catches the totality of a world at war: 'The world was sliding rapidly towards night like a torpedoed liner.' When he wrote this, Greene would have remembered his recent voyage to West Africa, when there was a constant danger of being sunk by a torpedo.

Like Greene's other earlier novels, *The Ministry of Fear* presents many cinematic effects. It was made into a film by Fritz Lang, but the experience of reading it recalls the favourite devices of the director whose work Greene disliked, Alfred Hitchcock. The tortuous plot turns round the search for what Hitchcock called a 'McGuffin', a small arbitrary object of immense significance that has been lost and must be found. In this case it is a reel of microfilm containing material of great national importance that a Nazi spy ring is after. This object is concealed in a cake that Rowe inadvertently acquires by fortuitously guessing its correct weight at the fête, though it was not intended for him. The opposition make great efforts to retrieve it and Rowe becomes one of Greene's hunted men. Greene indulges his taste for the grotesque in portraying the agents of the opposition. One of them is described as 'dark and dwarfish and twisted in his enormous shoulders with infantile paralysis', a vintage period description. Another is a female fortune-teller and spiritualist medium, who frames Rowe for a murder he has not committed. He loses his memory and is kidnapped and confined in a luxurious private clinic in a rural setting, run by a handsome and authoritative elderly doctor who, as it eventually appears, is quite mad. After various wild adventures set against the background of the ruined city and nightly air raids the right side, more or less, triumphs. The mortality rate is high, even for one of Greene's entertainments; once more the stage is littered with corpses, and Greene comments with some satisfaction, 'It had been a massacre on an Elizabethan scale.' One of the dead villains is a personable young Austrian refugee. His sister, Hilfe, though, is anti-Nazi, and Rowe becomes attached to her. The novel ends with a coming together that is even bleaker than the conclusion of *The Confidential Agent*: 'He tried tentatively a phrase, "My dear, my dear, I am so happy", and heard with infinite tenderness her prompt and guarded reply, "I am too". It seemed to him that after all one could exaggerate the value of happiness'.

Greene took the title of *The Ministry of Fear* from a poem by Wordsworth, and the novel has a further literary dimension. At the fête Rowe buys a second-hand copy of *The Little Duke*, a children's book by Charlotte M. Yonge, first published in 1854, and phrases from this work appear as epigraphs to the separate chapters of *The Ministry of Fear*. *The Little Duke* is a charming and readable though sentimental story, set in a remote era of French history, Normandy in the tenth century. The eponymous character, Richard, becomes Duke of Normandy as a small boy after his father is murdered. He is kidnapped by the French king and after various adventures is rescued by a loyal retainer. He grows up to be a good ruler, practising Christian forgiveness rather than the old Norse ethic of revenge, and is great-grandfather to William the Conqueror. The book has no obvious relation to Greene's novel, and the epigraphs are merely tags without thematic resonance. Greene's interest in Yonge's story remains private, though Victorian novels were very popular in wartime England for their escapist appeal. He may have been in joking vein, using the extracts from *The Little Duke* like a collage artist inserting bits of a text into a painting to point a contrast. *The Ministry of Fear* is a preposterous story, even allowing for its genre. But it is sharply written and conveys a strong sense of the physical reality and prevailing sensibility of London in the Blitz. At the same time, it is a vehicle for Greene's obsessions, and familiar images recur: the potting shed, the island in the lake, the green baize door, the temptation of suicide. Rowe had killed his wife out of pity, and the danger of pity is a recurring theme. It looks forward to Greene's next novel, *The Heart of the Matter*, in which Major Scobie is entirely undone by pity. *The Ministry of Fear* ends the first phase of Greene's career, when his ideal was what he called the poetic novel, rich in metaphor, often melodramatic, peopled by types and archetypes, grotesques and humours rather than 'rounded' fictional creations, which can be read like a poetic drama, or a dramatic poem.

NOTES

1. Julian Maclaren-Ross, *Memoirs of the Forties* (Harmondsworth, 1984), 25.

4
Brighton

GREENE originally thought that *Brighton Rock* would be an 'entertainment'. He changed his mind before the book was published, though not in time to stop the first American edition from being so described on the title page. Its roots in popular fiction are evident, both the classical detective story and the tough, fast-moving thriller on the American model. It also provides a mode of fictional mass-observation; it is immersed in the social behaviour and the sights, sounds and smells of Brighton on a few days of early summer in the mid-1930s. And it is the first of his novels to introduce overtly Catholic themes; among other things it is a moral fable about sin and damnation.

The novel opens forcefully: 'Hale knew, before he had been in Brighton three hours, that they meant to murder him. With his inky fingers and his bitten nails, his manner cynical or nervous, anybody could tell he didn't belong—belong to the early summer sun, the cool Whitsun wind off the sea, the holiday crowd.' The reasons why Charles Hale, also known as Fred, is in Brighton, and why he is afraid of being murdered, plunge one into the intricacies of the plot, which concerns the rivalry between Brighton racecourse gangs. A gang-leader called Kite has been killed on St Pancras Station by men working for the powerful Mr Colleoni; his death was not intended, but a slashing with razors got out of hand. Hale, a journalist, was in some way responsible for his death, having betrayed Kite's movements to his assailants. Kite's gang was taken over by Pinkie Brown, a strange, charismatic youth of 17, who venerated Kite for having rescued him from a hopeless existence in the slums of Brighton and set him up in, so to speak, a respectable criminal career. Now he is determined on revenge. (There is a reference to the death of Kite in *A Gun for Sale*, the only occasion on which Greene made a Balzacian or Trollopian link between his novels. There Raven says that he cut Kite's throat, though the circumstances are rather different from those described in *Brighton Rock*. Raven is like a crude early draft of Pinkie, but the death of Kite puts them on different sides.)

Hale is in Brighton as part of a publicity stunt for his newspaper. Under the name 'Kolley Kibber' (derived from the eighteenth-century poet and dramatist Colley Cibber) he follows a fixed itinerary, which has been published in the paper, and conceals small cards along the route. Anyone who finds one can claim a modest prize. His photograph has also been published, and someone who challenges him with the right form of words is awarded £10, a substantial sum in those days. The published itinerary makes it easy for Pinkie's gang to track him, and when Hale catches sight of one of them he feels he is doomed. He thinks he will be safer in the company of a woman and he picks up Ida Arnold, a cheerful, blowsy blonde divorcee who is in Brighton for the Whitsun Bank Holiday. She likes him, and they spend time in a pub together. He does not want her to leave him, but she insists that she must briefly visit the ladies' toilet at the entrance to the pier. She is gone for only a few minutes, but when she reappears Hale has vanished. Later his body is discovered in a shelter nearly a mile away by the West Pier, which was on his route. An inquest decides that he died of heart failure, but Ida is not satisfied. She had sensed that Hale was in a state of mortal fear, and she cannot understand how he got so far away in a few minutes. Ida senses there is something suspicious about the case, and starts to play the amateur detective. The reader follows her in her inquiries, which point to a mystery that is never finally resolved. Hale has indeed been abducted by the gang during the few minutes he was alone, and, it appears, was killed by Pinkie. But the post-mortem is correct in finding that death was caused by a coronary thrombosis.

Ida is consumed by the need to establish the truth about Hale's death. She returns to Brighton and uses her charms to persuade a police inspector to let her see the post-mortem report, though as far as he is concerned the case is closed. She notices that there is a description of bruising on the upper arms, which could indicate that Hale has been forcibly abducted, but the inspector says the bruises were probably caused by jostling in the holiday crowds, which Ida doubts. Pinkie's associates Cubitt, Dallow, and Spicer are also bothered by the inquest. Spicer says, 'That verdict sort of shook us all. What did they mean by it? We *did* kill him Pinkie?' Pinkie, also known as the Boy, seems untroubled, but Spicer goes on worrying. 'It was the medical evidence that upset him: "death from natural causes", when with his own eyes he'd seen the Boy . . . It was fishy, it wasn't straight.' We never do know what Spicer saw the Boy do, but Ida, firmly on the case, is collecting evidence. Later in the novel, when she is interrogating Cubitt, he suddenly bursts out, 'I can't see a piece of Brighton Rock without...', but refuses to say any more. Other clues suggest that Hale was killed in a small underground shop selling Brighton rock near the Palace Pier. We do not know how Hale died, but we know when he died. As a clock strikes half past one Ida comes out of the Ladies and finds that Hale has vanished. At 1.45 Pinkie is in a shooting booth on the pier and is at pains to confirm the time with the stallholder, who insists that the clock is right: 'It doesn't stand for any phoney alibis.' Just before 1.50 Pinkie is in a nearby tea-room and by 1.55 he is joined by the rest of the gang, whom he rebukes for being late. ' "Don't

take on so," Cubitt said. "'All you'd got to do was come straight across" ',
presumably from the shop where Pinkie had murdered Hale,
some time between 1.30 and 1.45. Dallow and Cubitt have taken his
body in their old car and deposited it in the shelter near the West
Pier, where 'Kolley Kibber' was supposed to be. If anyone had spot-
ted them, they could have said that Hale was ill or drunk. Pinkie is
at pains to establish an alibi, and Spicer has been distributing Hale's
cards along his route. He makes what proves to be a fatal error by
leaving one in Snow's restaurant, where he is seen by the young
waitress Rose. This leads to a central strand in the plot. When
Pinkie begins to feel threatened by Ida's investigations he resolves
to marry Rose, since in law a wife cannot give evidence against her
husband.

A consensus has emerged amongst critics about the way in which
Hale died. It was, I believe, first stated by David G. Wright in an
article in *The Explicator* in 1983; he argues that Hale was killed by
having a stick of rock rammed down his throat, which then set off a
heart attack. He refers to 'the grotesque oral rape of Hale with a
stick of rock'. This explanation has been accepted by later critics;
Michael Shelden is very specific: 'In the end Pinkie and his gang
have no difficulty in trapping Hale and taking his life with the
perfect weapon. By shoving a long stick of "Brighton Rock" down
his throat, they are able to kill him and dispose of the weapon at the
same time. The hard stick of sugar slowly dissolves in the body, and
after the police find Hale, they assume that he died a natural
death.'[1] Shelden is reading inattentively. The police did not merely
assume that Hale died a natural death; a post-mortem proved it.
And the idea that a stick of rock would dissolve and leave no trace is
implausible to anyone with childhood memories of such things, how
hard they are and how long they take to be sucked away (American
readers with no experience of seaside rock may be forgiven the
errors, but English ones should have realized). Furthermore, such

an 'oral rape' would have certainly left lacerations to the mouth and throat that the post-mortem would have revealed; there is no suggestion in the text that the investigation is incorrect, even though, as Ida believes, there is more to Hale's death than the heart attack it identifies. Ida makes a shrewd guess about the course of events: 'They took Fred down under the parade, into one of those little shops and strangled him—least they would have strangled him, but his heart gave out first . . . They strangled a dead man.' Strangulation would have left marks on Hale's neck that the post–mortem would have detected. But, as Ida concludes, however Hale was 'killed', he was already dead. The puzzle runs through the story, baffling the gangsters and Ida and several generations of read-ers. One might adopt a modified version of the 'oral rape' theory, by saying that Pinkie started to ram the rock down Hale's throat but before he had got very far—that is, not far enough to cause lacera-tions—his victim collapsed and died of a heart attack. That is a tidy but lame explanation, which just about covers the appearances, but I am not convinced by it. There might be no complete and final explanation, of the kind that is delivered at the end of the classical detective novel; in this respect *Brighton Rock* would be what later theorists called an 'indecipherable' text, like the French *nouveaux romans* of the 1950s. Greene, that notorious joker, might have scattered clues in the form of cryptic references and unfinished sentences about what happened to Hale but withheld a convincing final explanation.

I have discussed the plot of *Brighton Rock* in some detail in order to get it out of the way; new readers have to grapple with it, but it is the least interesting part of the story. Considered as a novel, *Brighton Rock* combines realism and poetry and shows an impressive development in Greene's talent. His earlier novels and entertainments tended to be episodic and improvisatory, with random brilliant moments that the novelist was content to capture and present as and when they occurred. *Brighton Rock*, though, is firmly structured in ways that go beyond the detective-story plot. Greene effectively deploys what Henry James recommended as the 'scenic method' by presenting his narrative as a succession of scenes that follow the unities of time and space, and uses free indirect style to move in and out of his characters' consciousness. The opening section is a good representative example: it begins with Hale moving through the streets of Brighton as 'Kolley Kibber', encountering Pinkie in a pub, picking up Ida, and then vanishing whilst she is in the Ladies at the Palace Pier. Apart from a couple of episodes with Ida in London, the action is confined to Brighton, with recurring foci: the tearoom on the Palace Pier, Snow's Restaurant on the Front, the shabby boarding-house on Montpellier Road occupied by Pinkie and his followers, the plush Cosmopolitan Hotel where Mr Colleoni is in residence. There are occasional visits elsewhere: the scrubby countryside beyond Peacehaven; the slum where Rose's parents live, the house of the shady solicitor Mr Prewitt near the railway viaduct.*

The novel shows Greene's keen ear for speech as well as his sharp eye for significant visual detail. He convincingly catches the language and tone of the mostly lower-class characters, though there are some eccentric elements; Pinkie and the gangsters habitually refer to women as 'buers' or 'polonies', archaic slang even in 1938. There are many examples of the imagistic urban poetry which had marked Greene's descriptions of London. In a passage such as this the poetry appears in the social observation that lies behind the

---

* In this use of topography Greene illustrates, on a small scale, the social zoning of urban areas discussed by Franco Moretti in *Atlas of the European Novel 1800–1900* (London, 1999). He had done something similar and more extensive with London in *It's a Battlefield*.

melodramatic action, like the detailed background of an early Renaissance painting:

It was quite dark now: the coloured lights were on all down the Hove front. They walked slowly past Snow's, past the Cosmopolitan. An aeroplane flying low burred out to sea, a red light vanishing. In one of the glass shelters an old man struck a match to light his pipe and showed a man and a girl cramped in the corner. A wail of music came off the sea. They turned up through Norfolk Square towards Montpellier Road: a blonde with Garbo cheeks paused to powder on the steps up to the Norfolk bar. A bell tolled for someone dead and a gramophone in a basement played a hymn. (part 6, 2)

It is an account that can be called cinematic, subject to the reservations I mentioned in a previous chapter. It is also literary: 'A wail of music came off the sea' (presumably from the West Pier) recalls 'This music crept by me upon the waters', the line from *The Tempest* that Eliot inserted into *The Waste Land*. And 'wail' may be an echo of another poetic novelist; in Scott Fitzgerald's *The Great Gatsby*, 'All night the saxophones wailed the hopeless comment of the "Beale Street Blues"'. The references to the aeroplane and the blonde with Garbo cheeks confirm the modernity of the scene. Elsewhere in the novel the poetry is conveyed in elaborate metaphors, which sometimes go beyond the baroque to the surrealist, as when the 16-year old Rose, just married to Pinkie, reacts angrily to Ida's interrogation: 'The bony and determined face stared back at her: all the fight there was in the world lay there—warships cleared for action and bombing fleets took flight between the set eyes and the stubborn mouth. It was like the map of a campaign marked with flags.' Greene may be drawing on the rapid images of a newsreel film, reflecting the common concern with a looming war. But in that context the effect recalls a painting by Dali or Magritte. *Brighton Rock* often shows a degree of rhetorical organization that is closer to poetry than to modern fictional prose, as in the triadic grouping where nouns or phrases are linked in threes: 'This was real now: the boy, the razor cut, life going out with the blood in pain: not the deck chairs and the permanent waves, the miniature cars tearing round the curve on the Palace Pier'; 'his pallid face peered dimly back at him full of pride from the mirror, over the ewer, the soap-dish, the basin of stale water.' (K.W. Gransden has pointed out that in classical rhetoric this device is known as 'tricolon in asyndeton'.)

It is understandable that when *Brighton Rock* is not read simply as a thriller it is likely to be regarded as a tough, obsessively observed story of Brighton low life in the 1930s. As with my reading of Greene's earlier novels, I believe that, though the realistic elements are evident, they compete with very different qualities. This is particularly true of the characterization. The narrative is dominated by Pinkie, and from the beginning it is evident that he is unlike the characters of mainstream novels, who are immediately recognizable and believable, and yet capable of changing and surprising one. Indeed, from the beginning he is presented as something other: 'A boy of about seventeen watched him from the door—a shabby smart suit, the cloth too thin for much wear, a face of starved intensity, a kind of hideous and unnatural pride'; 'his grey eyes had an effect of heartlessness like an old man's in which human feeling has died'; 'Hale looked up at the grey inhuman seventeen-year old eyes'; 'From behind he looked younger than he was in his thin ready-made suit a little too big for him, but when you met him face to face he looked older, the slatey eyes were touched with the annihilating eternity from which he had come and to which he went'. These descriptions have a power and precision that are new in Greene's writing, and they make Pinkie seem other than human— 'unnatural', 'heartless', 'inhuman'—culminating in the extraordinary phrase, 'the annihilating eternity from which he had come and to which he went'. This prefigures Pinkie's violent and horrible end, but more than that, it presents him as a dark angel, not subject to time and human limitations. Pinkie is an archetypal figure, and *Brighton Rock*, for all its extensive realistic dimensions, has to be read as fabular fiction. Pinkie loses plausibility if one takes it simply as a work of social realism akin to Patrick Hamilton's novels of English life in the 1930s. The idea advanced by Maria Couto that Pinkie is just a juvenile delinquent, the brutalized victim of a slum childhood, will not stand up.[2] Greene endorsed Couto's account, which I take to be an indication of his readiness in later years to reinterpret his early work in the light of his subsequent views; it may also reflect his tendency to agree with an interlocutor whom he found sympathetic. If Pinkie is a dark angel, he has taken on human attributes, though even then they tend to make him seem inhuman. He follows his mentor Kite in not smoking or drinking alcohol—he has a taste for grapefruit squash—and he is a virgin, whose horror of sex is fuelled by childhood memories of 'the frightening weekly exercise of his parents which he watched from his single bed'.

Although *Brighton Rock* is essentially a fable, it draws effectively on the conventions and situations of traditional realism. There is a particularly good brief scene where Pinkie goes to see the rich elderly gangster Mr Colleoni, who has invited him to call on him in his suite in the Cosmopolitan Hotel, to discuss a possible merger of their enterprises. Colleoni is surprised that Kite's successor is so young and offers him a job. Pinkie keeps a bold face on things; like many socially aspiring young men in nineteenth- and twentieth-century novels he is impressed by a display of wealth and power but tries not to show it; he refuses Colleoni's offer of a drink and a cigar, and of employment, and says he wants to go on running his own gang. The atmosphere is lightened by an inconsequential exchange: '"Napoleon the Third used to have this room," Mr. Colleoni said, "and Eugenie". "Who was she?" "Oh," Mr Colleoni said vaguely, "one of those foreign polonies." ' Mr Colleoni may not be an emperor, but he has a great deal of power: 'sitting there in the rich Victorian room, with the gold lighter in his pocket and the cigar-case on his lap, he looked as a man might look who owned the whole world, the whole visible world that is, the cash registers and policemen and prostitutes, Parliament and the laws which say "this is Right and this is Wrong".' Here Greene pulls away from the conventions of realism to present the gangster as a quasi-mythic figure; in looking as if he owned the whole world Mr Colleoni recalls the Devil tempting Christ. This scene is also interesting as evidence of how Greene toned down his early anti-Semitism. In the original text of 1938 Pinkie's arrival at the hotel is described thus: 'A little Jewess sniffed at him bitchily and then talked him over with another little Jewess on a settee. Mr Colleoni came across an acre of deep carpet from the Louis Seize writing room, walking on tiptoe in glacé shoes. He was a small Jew with a neat round belly; he wore a grey double-breasted waistcoat, and his eyes gleamed like raisins.' (The raisins may recall another Jew, Carleton Myatt in *Stamboul Train*.) In the revised post-war text the Jewesses have become 'little bitches', and Colleoni is merely 'small with a neat round belly'. Towards the end of his discussion with Pinkie, the 1938 text has 'His old semitic face showed few emotions but a mild amusement, a mild friendliness'; this becomes 'His old Italian face . . .' If Colleoni was originally a Jew, it is odd that Greene gave him an Italian name, though one with associations of power. Bartolomeo Colleoni was the famous *condottiere* whose equestrian statue by Verrochio stands prominently in the Campo Santi Giovanni e Paolo in Venice.

If there are times when *Brighton Rock* uses the conventions of the realistic novel, there are others when it invokes older literary forms. Shelden refers to the medieval morality plays that Greene admired, where characters embody concepts or qualities rather than complexities of thought and feeling; he remarks that many of Greene's characters are 'best understood as poetic abstractions whose moods are more important than their motives' and says that 'Pinkie acts Revenge with terrifying skill'. This is true, but it is in later plays that he would be most at home, if that is the word for it. It is not hard to imagine the central action of the novel lifted out of England in the 1930s and inserted into the sinister Italian settings of Elizabethan and Jacobean tragedy. Much would fit in easily: the gang warfare, the ingenious forms of murder, the betrayals, the casual cruelty, the bewildered pathos of the young and innocent victim Rose, Pinkie's appalling end. Here he would, in every sense, be in his element; a successor to the Revenge of the morality plays, but also what the Elizabethans called a Machiavel, or 'match-evil', who was deliberately wicked, cunning, energetic, and cruel, like Marlowe's Barabas, Shakespeare's Iago and Edmund, and Webster's Flamineo and Bosola. Literary references or allusions are woven into the text. Pinkie, lying on his bed and pulling the wings off a flying insect, then brushing it away, is enacting Gloucester's simile in *King Lear*:

> As flies to wanton boys are we to the gods,
> They kill us for their sport. (IV. i)

Towards the end of his career of crime Pinkie says, 'It's no good stopping now. We got to go on', and we recall *Macbeth*:

> I am in blood
> Steeped in so far, should I wade no more
> Returning were as tedious as go o'er. (III. iv)

In Pinkie's last interview with Mr Prewitt, the broken-down solicitor, rather the worse for drink, scatters references to *Hamlet*, and quotes Marlowe's Mephistopheles: 'Why, this is hell, nor am I out of it.' (An early reference to Pinkie had adapted Wordsworth to read, 'Hell lay about him in his infancy'.)

To repeat a passage I previously quoted from Greene's *British Dramatists*: 'in Tourneur and the earlier Webster we are in the company of men who would really seem to have been lost in the dark night of the soul if they had enough religious sense to feel despair: the world is all there is, and the world is violent, mad, miserable and without point.' (Greene no doubt assumes, as Eliot did, that Tourneur wrote *The Revenger's Tragedy*, rather than Middleton, as is now believed.) This sounds like Pinkie's world, one in which he tries to trap others, particularly Rose, enacting Greene's recurring preoccupation with the betrayal of innocence. But Pinkie, unlike the Jacobean lost souls, does have enough religious sense to feel despair and to be concerned with damnation.

This consideration points to *Brighton Rock*'s most controversial aspect: its significance and reputation as a Catholic novel. Greene had become a Catholic in 1926, when he was working as an apprentice journalist in Nottingham. He was engaged to Vivien Dayrell-Browning, herself a Catholic convert, and as he records in *A Sort of Life* he started taking instruction in Catholic doctrine from a Fr Trollope, not with a view to entering the Church, as he was a convinced atheist, but in order to find out something about what she believed. Then, in January 1926, following what devout believers would see as a sudden influx of grace, Greene became convinced of the probable existence of God, and the rest of the process followed. He was received into the Catholic Church: 'I remember very strongly the nature of my emotion as I walked away from the Cathedral: there was no joy in it at all, only a sombre apprehension.' In Greene's fiction before *Brighton Rock* there are no overt indications of the author's religion, though there are possible hints of it. In *Stamboul Train*, the Communist Richard Czinner, on his way to take part in a revolution, remembers his Catholic boyhood and feels a desire for Confession: 'The priest's face turned away, the raised fingers, the whisper of a dead tongue, seemed to him suddenly as beautiful, as infinitely desirable and as hopelessly lost as youth and first love in the corner of the viaduct wall.' In *It's a Battlefield* Jules hears Mass at the French church in Soho: 'The priest addressed the congregation in French on the subject of sin; the word *péché, péché, péché*, held down his sermon like so many brass tacks driven into a wood coffin. The restaurateurs of Soho folded their hands and translated the term into *"femme, femme, femme"*, *"grue, grue, grue"*.'

Catholicism is more explicit in Greene's essays and reviews of the 1930s. In 'Frederick Rolfe: Edwardian Inferno', a review of A. J. A. Symons's *The Quest for Corvo*, he dwells with fascination on the eccentric man of letters—otherwise known as Baron Corvo—whose career was a lifelong quarrel with the Catholic Church, which, quite rightly, refused to consider him a suitable candidate for the priesthood. Greene throws out remarks which anticipate the themes of his Catholic novels: 'The greatest saints have been men with more than a normal capacity for evil, and the most vicious men have sometimes narrowly evaded sanctity'. He concludes the piece by making Rolfe sound like a Greene character: 'He would be a priest or nothing, so nothing it had to be and he was not ashamed to live on his friends; if he could not have Heaven, he would have Hell, and the last footprints seem to point unmistakably towards the Inferno.' In a review of Eliot's *After Strange Gods* Greene wrote, 'To be a Catholic (in Mr Eliot's case an Anglo-Catholic) is to believe in the Devil, and why, if the Devil exists, he should not work through contemporary literature, it is hard to understand.'[3] Greene's essay 'Henry James: The Religious Aspect' is a carefully argued study of a novelist whom he greatly admired, though in the end it is more revealing about Greene than about James. Greene opposes the common opinion that James was a writer who not only lacked religious belief but had no capacity for religious feeling. He shows that James always had a sympathetic interest in the Catholic Church. This was evident in his response to the aesthetic aspects of Catholicism: the music, the art, the appeal of ritual and ceremony. At a deeper level there was James's attachment to the Catholic

BRIGHTON

practice of praying for the dead, evident in what Greene calls 'that
beautiful and ridiculous story "The Altar of the Dead"'. But he
finds James's religious sense most profoundly expressed in his
sense of evil, which Greene believes attracted him to the Catholic
Church. The Church took Hell seriously, and at Mass prayers
were said for deliverance from evil spirits 'wandering through the
world for the ruin of souls'. Greene finds such spirits in 'The Turn
of the Screw', where, in the ghostly apparitions of Peter Quint and
Miss Jessel, 'is the explicit breath of Hell'. Greene sees other James
characters, the betrayers of innocence, as candidates for damnation. He quotes from Eliot's essay on Baudelaire: ' "The worst that
can be said of most of our malefactors, from statesmen to thieves, is
that they are not men enough to be damned". This worst cannot be
said of James's characters: both Densher and the Prince have on
their faces the flush of the flames' (I have corrected a slight mis-
quotation in the Eliot passage). Greene envisages a very traditional
Hell, echoed at the death of Pinkie: 'He looked half his size, doubled
up in appalling agony: it was as if the flames had literally got him'.
At that time Greene was very much a hellfire Catholic, though
years later he told Marie-Françoise Allain, 'I have never believed in
hell'. A writer, like anyone else, is entitled to change his mind, but
this remark looks like either denial or amnesia.

Greene was fusing Catholic doctrine, as it was often understood
at that period, with his personal mythology, which was much concerned with betrayal and loss, cruelty and evil. Shelden has written
of 'Henry James: The Religious Aspect', 'the only religious aspects
that Greene discusses are hell, the devil, damnation and evil'. In the
first phase of his career it appears that these were the aspects, out of
all the great totality of Catholic belief and practice, that his imagination highlighted and which were important to him as literary
resources. In *Ways of Escape* Greene writes that following his con-
version his Catholicism was a matter of dutiful formal observance,

and that it was not until he went to Mexico in 1938 to witness the persecution of religion there that his religion became emotionally important to him, as he described in *The Lawless Roads*. But *Brighton Rock*, which he completed before he travelled, suggests that the process was already under way, and involved more than a sense that, as he claimed, he had finally got to know enough about Catholicism to introduce it into a novel. *Brighton Rock* is too intense and obsessive a narrative to be merely the product of a calm extension of subject matter.

Eliot's reading of Baudelaire seems to have shown him the possibilities of damnation as a topic in a modern novel, as it had been in Elizabethan and Jacobean drama (as when Hamlet refrains from killing Claudius whilst he is saying his prayers in case he escapes Hell). Before the passage quoted by Greene, Eliot wrote, 'It is better, in a paradoxical way, to do evil than to do nothing: at least we exist.' John Carey, a perceptive but severe critic of *Brighton Rock*, takes understandable objection to Eliot's sentiment: 'This appalling sentence leaves out of account, we notice, the effect of evil on its victims. A murderer, like Greene's Pinkie, could hardly be said to make things "better" for those he kills, even if he enhances his own spiritual reality.'[4] Put in such terms, Carey's objection is unanswerable. One can only say that this is a literary idea that makes subjective sense to a writer and which should not, indeed cannot, be enacted in the real world. In Eliot's case it relates to those wandering lost souls at the beginning of the *Inferno* who were not fit for either salvation or damnation; their indeterminate state was deeply interesting and personally affecting to Eliot. Insofar as Greene adopted this idea he may have misunderstood and diminished it, as is liable to happen if we try to take over someone else's preoccupations.

Baudelaire and Eliot and Greene all draw on the potent concept of evil. Centuries of Christian homiletics, moral theology, and iconography have left believers with the conviction that evil is a mighty force in the world, and that there is a tough continuing battle between God and the Devil for the souls of men. As a result orthodox Christianity has been continually threatened by the kind of popular Manichaeism that the idea of evil, if only slightly misinterpreted, can easily imply. In a purer theological air, evil is not positive at all, but a lack, an absence; Aquinas believed it was a privation of the good proper to something, as blindness might be to the good of the eye. But this calm conviction offers little imaginative purchase either to preachers condemning sin or to imaginative writers exploiting human dramas.

Pinkie identifies Rose as a Catholic when he notices a rosary in her handbag. He tells her that he is one too; as a boy he sang in a church choir, though now he no longer goes to Mass.

'But you believe, don't you,' Rose implored him, 'you think it's all true?'

'Of course it's true,' the Boy said. 'What else could there be?' he went scornfully on. 'Why,' he said,' 'it's the only thing that fits. These atheists, they don't know nothing. Of course there's Hell. Flames and damnation,' he said with his eyes on the dark shifting water and the lightning at the lamps going out above the black struts of the Palace Pier, 'torments'.

'And Heaven too,' Rose said with anxiety, while the rain fell interminably on.

'Oh, maybe,' the Boy said, 'maybe'. (part 2, 1)

Pinkie, like Frederick Rolfe in Greene's interpretation, is surer of Hell than of Heaven. Rose is more orthodox; though well aware of the danger of Hell she understands Heaven as the true goal of the believer. Later Pinkie says to one of his gang, *'Credo in unum Satanum'*, implausibly adapting the Latin words of the Creed to show that he is a Satanist rather than a Catholic, a dark angel not a teenage criminal. We learn that as a boy he wanted to be a priest. Like the original Satan he has fallen from high spiritual possibilities; the references to Pinkie's 'pride' confirm his Luciferian affinities. After his death the old priest says to Rose, *'Corruptio optimi est pessima'*.

George Orwell was exasperated by all this, remarking that in *Brighton Rock*,

the central situation is incredible, since it presupposes that the most brutishly stupid person can, merely by having been brought up a Catholic, be capable of great intellectual subtlety. Pinkie, the race-course gangster, is a species of satanist, while his still more limited girl friend understands and even states the difference between the categories 'right and wrong' and 'good and evil'.[5]

Orwell's remark is at the same time perceptive and wrong-headed, and it shows how the demonic Pinkie cannot be regarded as a credible character in a traditional novel. He is wrong in describing him as 'brutishly stupid', for Pinkie is clearly intelligent; like the Elizabethan Machiavel, he is cunning, shrewd, and manipulative; he also responds to music. But Orwell is alert to the way in which Pinkie and Rose represent for Greene the exclusiveness that English Catholicism derived from centuries of isolation and legal disabilities. Pinkie and Rose, dismissing Ida as 'ignorant', are almost echoing the Catholic polemicist Hilaire Belloc: 'It is so with the whole matter—of finance, of health, of all life, of death, of dereliction and bereavement—*all* are one thing in the Catholic air, and wholly different and incomparably worse in quality in the atmosphere of whatever is not Catholic.'[6]

The opposition between Good and Evil, on the one hand, and Right and Wrong on the other, has become a crux in discussions of the novel. Its Catholic admirers regard the former as pointing to authentic spiritual values and the latter as reflecting a godless humanism, and have assumed that Greene sees it that way. His hostile critics have reversed the emphasis, condemning the religious exclusiveness that rejects so much human value. In fact, the distinction reflects a range of religious attitudes rather than an absolute opposition between the religious and the humanistic. Many believers would regard a faltering, inchoate sense of right and wrong as an imperfect apprehension of the values implied in good and evil, not something opposed to them (and, as I have suggested, 'evil' is itself a problematical concept).

Ida Arnold talks about 'right and wrong' and is condemned as 'ignorant' by Pinkie and Rose, the upholders of Catholic mystery. She is an engaging character, modelled on Mae West, liking male company and a glass of port or a Guinness; something of a caricature, but that is acceptable in an essentially fabular narrative. In *Ways of Escape* Greene refers to her as 'the barmaid who so obstinately refused to come alive'. In fact, there is no specific description in the novel of Ida as a barmaid, though she likes being on the customers' side of the bar; she tells Fred Hale that she lives 'from hand to mouth'. (Greene could be inaccurate about what was in his earlier novels; looking back on *It's a Battlefield*, he refers to the prison that the Assistant Commissioner visits as Wormwood Scrubs, but he locates it south of the river, somewhere near Clapham Junction.) Ida might not have come alive as much as some of Greene's characters, such as the memorable Minty, but she has sufficient vitality to play the role of detective, and to embody, like a figure in a morality play, that God-given attribute, a thirst for justice; she is determined to discover the truth about Hale's death. Greene wrote that one should not assume that he shared the ideas of his Catholic characters, not even their Catholic ideas; to which one can add that 'Catholic ideas' are by no means clear-cut entities, especially when they have been transformed into fiction. What Greene believed about the issues he raised in *Brighton Rock* is not at all certain. His friend Shirley Hazzard has written, 'There was ... an authorial distance that could make it hard to establish where his sympathies lay—in *Brighton Rock*, for instance.'[7]

Hazzard's remark is a corrective to the view of John Carey, who admires *Brighton Rock* but fits it into his thesis that much modern literature is inspired by contempt for the masses. Pursuing this thesis, Carey tends to misread the novel. He refers to the long account of the race-going crowds that opens Part 4. It is a brilliant piece of writing, a cross-cutting montage of juxtaposed images; the people making their way to the races, in cars, taxis, buses, or on foot are contrasted with the offspring of the rich: 'In the great public-school grounds above the sea the girls trooped solemnly out to hockey.' Greene avoids class prejudice; if the plebeian racegoers are seen in less than human terms—'they surged like some natural and irrational migration of insects up and down the front'—so are the girls at the posh school—'stout goalkeepers padded like armadillos'. The tone is detached, not hostile, and the author responds to the excitement and vitality of the scene. Grahame Smith, a more sympathetic critic than Carey, comments, 'the dehumanising simile of people as insects should be set against the sympathy for mundane lives contained within the narrative itself: "The odds on Black Boy had shortened, nothing could ever make life quite the same again after the rash bet of a fiver on Merry Monarch."'[8] Both Smith and Carey refer to the dashing appearance of Ida Arnold in the procession:

A scarlet racing model, a tiny rakish car which carried about it the atmosphere of innumerable roadhouses, of totsies gathered round swimming pools, of furtive encounters in by-lanes off the Great North Road, wormed through the traffic with incredible dexterity. The sun caught it: it winked as far as the dining-hall windows of the girls' school. It was crammed tight: a woman sat on a man's knee, and another man clung on the running board as it swayed and hooted and cut in and out uphill towards the Downs. The woman was singing, her voice faint and disjointed through the horns, something traditional about brides and bouquets, something which went with Guinness and oysters, and the old Leicester Lounge, something out of place in the little bright racing car. (part 4, 1)

It is a passage which Greene's critics would agree on describing as cinematic; but the film it invokes would need to be a talkie, to catch Ida's singing, and in Technicolor to register the scarlet racing car. It provides a brilliant fusion of mass observation and imagistic poetry (with one of Greene's characteristic triads in the postpositional description of the 'tiny rakish car'). Commenting on the passage, Carey acknowledges that Greene has a sneaking sympathy for Ida, which undermines his thesis that she is no more than the object of a snobbish assault. He rightly says, 'her vitality is what drives the plot: without her investigations the story would not move forward.' Greene, I imagine, knew that too; all readers' sympathies must be with Ida in the final pages as she races to save Rose from Pinkie's terrible plan of a false suicide pact.

As he is driving her out to this fate Pinkie asks Rose what she is thinking; she replies, 'Life's not so bad.' He responds like a Jacobean villain in extremis: ' "Don't you believe it," he said. "I'll tell you what it is. It's gaol, it's not knowing where to get some money. Worms and cataract, cancer. You hear 'em shrieking from the upper windows—children being born. It's dying slowly." ' Rose's 'Life's not so bad', is, as Sherry has noted, the sort of thing that Ida would say. It also expresses a central Christian truth: in a fallen world, life is bad, but it is not *so* bad. There is always hope, which is what Pinkie denies. And right up to the moment when she is supposed to shoot herself, Rose clings to the hope of salvation, even though she wants to share damnation with Pinkie. It seems appropriate that she should be rescued by Ida.

Rose is one of Greene's familiar female types, the plucky waif. She is more of a victim than most, both of Pinkie's cruelty and of her own desperate love for him. She is believable, but she lacks the stature that her role requires; perhaps only Dostoevsky could have given it to her. After Pinkie's death, Rose's enduring Catholicism sends her to talk to a priest, though she does not want to make a conventional Confession. Indeed, she tells the old priest smelling of eucalyptus she wishes she had killed herself and gone to share damnation with Pinkie. Greene expresses it in an extraordinary, haunting image: 'She would have found the courage now to kill herself if she hadn't been afraid that somewhere in that obscure countryside of death they might miss each other—mercy operating somehow for one and not for the other.' The priest makes some reflections that may have been incomprehensible to Rose, but then tells her that if Pinkie had loved her it showed that there was some good in him. She has deluded herself that he had and she grasps this assurance. Soon after they were married he had gone to a shop where messages could be put on gramophone records, and told her that he recorded 'something loving'; in fact, it is an appalling outburst of hatred and repulsion. Rose has never heard the message since she does not own a gramophone but at the end of the novel she is about to take it to someone who does and play it: 'She walked rapidly in the thin June sunlight towards the worst horror of all.' It is a melodramatic rather than a tragic conclusion, pointing to the posthumous triumph of Pinkie's wickedness, and it has proved understandably troubling to many readers. In fact, the gratuitous emphasis on the final cruelty is a form of negative sentimentality, exploiting feeling for its own sake.

The priest's remarks to Rose touch directly on Greene's interest in damnation:

He said: 'There was a man, a Frenchman, you wouldn't know about him, my child, who had the same idea as you. He was a good man, a holy man, and he lived in sin all through his life, because he couldn't bear the idea that any soul could suffer damnation.' She listened with astonishment. He said: 'This man decided that if any soul was going to be damned, he would be damned too. He never took the sacraments, he never married his wife in church. I don't know, my child, but some people think he was—well, a saint. I think he died in what we are told is mortal sin—I'm not sure: it was in the war: perhaps…' He sighed and whistled, bending his old head. He said: 'You can't conceive, my child, nor can I or anyone—the appalling strangeness of the mercy of God.' (part 6, ii)

The Frenchman is Charles Péguy, whose ideas interested Greene. The priest is speaking in orthodox terms when he refers to the unknowable nature of God's mercy and says, 'The Church does not demand that we believe any soul is cut off from mercy.' This is true, but it means that we do not have to believe that anyone, however great a sinner, is necessarily damned; which is a different matter from opting for solidarity with those who are. For the orthodox believer, damnation is not something that is imposed—God wishes all humanity to be saved—but something that the impenitent sinner freely and deliberately wills. This merciful belief is less imaginatively striking than the familiar tradition, illustrated in Christian literature and art, that the damned are a vast number who will be bundled off to Hell at the Last Judgement.

Greene took from Péguy the idea, that recurs in later books, that there is something arbitrary about damnation, which could warrant siding with the victims, even suggesting a Promethean revolt against a tyrannical deity. We here touch on theological arguments about grace and predestination; the arbitrariness implies a Calvinist rather than a Catholic emphasis. A sense of damnation as a potentially attractive as well as a fearful fate permeated Greene's imagination at that stage of his career. However, the quality of *Brighton Rock* as a literary work does not depend on its theological dimensions. It derives from the power of the writing and observation, the poetry, the skilled mingling of genres, and above all the literally inhuman force of the central character. Pinkie, in his strength and youth and wickedness, is the kind of doomed hero that the Elizabethans called an 'overreacher'. Though he fits for much of the time into a realistic thriller, he does not belong there. Two of Greene's severest critics, John Carey and Michael Shelden, have each called *Brighton Rock* a masterpiece,[9] and I agree; I see it as his finest novel and among the outstanding works of British fiction in the first half of the twentieth century.

NOTES

1. M. Shelden, *Graham Greene* (London, 1994), 235.

2. Maria Couto, *Graham Greene: On the Frontier* (Basingstoke, 1988).

3. *Life and Letters*, April 1934.

4. John Carey, *The Intellectuals and the Masses* (London, 1992), 85

5. George Orwell, 'The Sanctified Sinner', in S. Hynes (ed.), *Graham Greene* (Englewood Cliffs, NJ, 1973), 105–9.

6. Hilaire Belloc, *Letters*, ed. Robert Speaight (London, 1958), 247.

7. S. Hazzard, *Greene on Capri* (London, 2000), 73.

8. Grahame Smith, *The Achievement of Graham Greene* (Brighton, 1986), 60.

9. Carey, *Intellectuals*, 83; M. Shelden, *Graham Greene* (London, 1994), 101.

5
Mexico

IN spring 1938, while *Brighton Rock* was still in the press, Greene went to Mexico. He had been commissioned by a publisher to write a book on the state of the Catholic Church in that country, where for several years it had been persecuted by a fiercely anti-religious government. He spent some weeks travelling in the remoter regions, often in great discomfort, and produced two of his best books. *The Lawless Roads*, the one he had been commissioned to write, is as much an autobiographical exploration as a survey of conditions in the country, while *The Power and the Glory* is one of his most popular novels, and at the same time one of the most profound. *The Lawless Roads* is a complex and artful text. It is very literary, drawing on Greene's extensive reading, but the prose is vivid, conveying physical sensations with painful immediacy. A lighter note sometimes appears, as when he discovers a community of Mexicans who are all called 'Graham' or 'Greene'. There is a strong Catholic emphasis: the narrator makes efforts to hear Mass and sometimes attends Benediction as well; he goes to Confession when he is moving into a dangerous phase of his journey, and he recites 'Hail Marys' when he is scared in a storm. Although there is a great gulf between the Catholicism of the Mexican Indians, with their strange and extravagant devotions, and that of the Oxford-educated English convert, he recognizes a community of faith with them. The tone is set by the long quotation from Newman which provides an epigraph to

The Lawless Roads. Newman reflects on the violent, disturbed, and seemingly hopeless condition of the world: 'What shall be said to this heart-piercing, reason-bewildering fact? I can only answer, that either there is no Creator, or this living society of men is in a true sense discarded from his presence . . . *if* there be a God, *since* there is a God, the human race is implicated in some terrible aboriginal calamity' (*Apologia Pro Vita Sua*, ch. 7. Present-day theologians would avoid referring to 'a God'). The calamity is Original Sin; Chesterton, in *Orthodoxy*, expressed a similar thought in less dramatic language: 'there had come into my mind a vague and vast impression that in some way all good was a remnant to be stored and held sacred out of some primordial ruin. Man had saved his good as Crusoe saved his goods: he had saved them from a wreck.'

The Prologue to *The Lawless Roads* is a forceful and elaborate piece of writing, which opens, not in Mexico, but in Berkhamsted, the small town in Hertfordshire where Greene grew up and where he attended the public school of which his father was headmaster. He evokes the motif of the 'green baize door' that recurs in his writing. This door separated the school, where Greene was a boarder during the week, from the family home to which he returned at weekends: 'There would be a slight smell of iodine from the matron's room, of damp towels from the changing rooms, of ink everywhere. Shut the door behind you again, and the world smelt differently again: books and fruit and eau-de-Cologne.' He grew up with an acute sense of a divided existence: 'How can life on a border be other than restless? You are pulled by different ties of hate and love.' Greene's unhappy schooldays were something he had in common with other writers of his generation who were educated at public schools and freely drew on them for literary material. Given the peculiarities of his divided existence, and his sensitivity to the bullying he endured as the Head's son, his experiences at school emphasized and directed the obsessions which coloured his imagination: 'And so faith came to one—shapelessly, without dogma, a presence above a croquet lawn; something associated with violence, cruelty, evil across the way. One began to believe in heaven because one believed in hell, but for a long while it was only hell one could picture with a certain intimacy.' Later, 'one began slowly, painfully, reluctantly to populate heaven'.

Greene switches from the Berkhamsted of his schooldays to the town as he had found it on a recent visit. He subjects it to a keen mass-observing survey, just as he had Brighton in his last novel, and repeats motifs and devices from *Brighton Rock*: the allusions to Wordsworth and Marlowe—'Hell lay about them in their infancy', 'Why, this is hell, nor am I out of it'—and the grim story of the pregnant adolescent girl who committed suicide with her boyfriend on a railway line, where their headless bodies were discovered. The suicide-pact recalls Pinkie's design on Rose. Greene imaginatively linked Brighton, Berkhamsted, and Mexico; all showed the marks of the 'terrible aboriginal calamity'. In chapter 7 of *The Lawless Roads* he noted, 'I dreamed that I had returned from Mexico to Brighton for one day, and then had to sail again immediately to Vera Cruz.'

After Berkhamsted, the Prologue then moves to Mexico, referring to the life and death of Fr Miguel Pro, a young Jesuit priest who had entered the country in July 1926 and secretly followed his priestly mission for a year and a half, saying Mass, hearing confessions and giving communion. Then he was caught, imprisoned, and shot. In describing Fr Pro, Greene refers to Edmund Campion, the Elizabethan Jesuit martyr—later canonized—whose mission and fate were similar. Greene had admiringly reviewed the biography of Campion that Evelyn Waugh published in 1935, and he drew on Fr Pro and Campion and other Jesuit martyrs in *The Power and the Glory*. Sherry says there is some evidence that the story of the 'whisky priest' was in Greene's mind before he went to Mexico, which need not be surprising: the forms of the imagination are always seeking material.

The last paragraph of the Prologue takes us to Greene's situation as a traveller to Mexico, but gets there via Berkhamsted, where he had lived on both sides of a frontier as a schoolboy: 'The great brick buildings rose at the end of the lawn against the sky—like the hotels in the United States which you can watch from Mexico leaning among the stars across the international bridge.' Greene spent some days on the American side of the bridge, waiting for transport into Mexico, as he describes in the first chapter of *The Lawless Roads*, which is called 'The Border'. Frontiers were personally important to Greene, but they were also a common motif in the English writing of the 1930s, as I have described elsewhere.* His journey, though he describes it with intense realism, has an archetypal quality which recalls the quests in famous modernist texts. Mexico is a federal state, and Catholicism was more tolerated in the capital and some provinces than in remoter areas. And it was to these areas, particularly Tabasco and Chiapas, where persecution was still active, that Greene was headed. He travelled by a variety of means: by train, bus, ship, plane, muleback, and on foot. He was resilient about the physical hardships of the journey, but he came to hate Mexico for its corruption and casual cruelty: 'No hope anywhere. I have never been in a country where you are more aware all the time of hate.' He may be alluding to Conrad's *Heart of Darkness* when he writes, 'One felt one was drawing near to the centre of something—if it was only of darkness and abandonment.' Greene refers elsewhere to Conrad's novel in his writing; there is a quotation from it near the beginning of *In Search of a Character*: ' "And this, also," said Marlow suddenly, "has been one of the dark places of the earth." ' Greene's official reason, or pretext, for his journey was a supposed wish to

---

* See 'Transformations of the Frontier' in my *Reading the Thirties* (London, 1978).

visit a famous set of pre-colonial ruins. He finally reaches them, though he is exhausted after his long ride on a mule and he takes little interest when he arrives. I am reminded of the moment in part V of *The Waste Land*, a poem for which Greene had a high regard, when the traveller, in 'this decayed hole among the mountains', finds 'tumbled graves' and an 'empty chapel' which is only 'the wind's home'. Mexico, for Greene, was 'a country to die in and leave ruins behind'.

Yet the Catholicism of the people, persisting in the face of terrible difficulties, was something positive that Greene clung to. He reflects after talking to a priest, 'What right had an English Catholic to bitterness or horror at human nature when this Mexican priest had none?' At times he finds human goodness. A ragged old man who lives in great poverty has no food to give Greene and his guide but he makes them coffee and gives up his earth bed to Greene. After the horrors of the journey, 'all that was left was an old man on the edge of starvation living in a hut with the rats, welcoming the strangers without a word of payment, gossiping gently in the dark. I felt myself back with the population of heaven.' Heaven could still make an occasional appearance in Greene's scheme of things. He was moved and fascinated by the faith of the Indians, which he acknowledged was blended with non-Christian elements. There is another suggestion of *The Waste Land*, when he writes, 'there was an even older world beyond the ridge; the ground sloped up again to where a grove of tall black crosses stood at all angles like wind-blown trees against the blackened sky. This was the Indian religion—a dark, tormented, magic cult.' These crosses deeply stirred Greene—they reappear in *The Power and the Glory*—and prompted searching and disturbing reflections on the nature of religion: 'here, in the mountainous strange world . . . Christianity went on its own frightening way. Magic, yes, but we are too apt to minimize the magic element in Christianity—the man raised from the dead, the devils cast out, the water turned into wine.' Greene was prepared to admit a place for magic in religious belief, though not the crude superstition that was often blended with popular Catholicism. Towards the end of his visit he spent time in the city of Las Casas, where the churches were closed but priests were tolerated and could say Mass in private houses. Greene was intrigued by talk of a 'miracle box' which was supposed to convey messages from St Michael and cure the sick, and had become the focus of a local cult. After some difficulty he got to see the box, which was an obvious tawdry fake: 'The Mass is forbidden in the churches; only in the secrecy of a private house can the daily genuine miracle be performed; but religion will out, and when it is suppressed it breaks its way through in strange and sometimes poisonous forms.'

Greene said that his visit to Mexico turned his Catholicism from a matter of conviction and observance to something deeper. There is no reason to doubt this, though, as I have remarked, in *Brighton Rock* he had begun exploiting the emotional possibilities of a version of Catholicism. One says 'a version' advisedly; religious belief is always likely to be affected by elements drawn from personal temperament and prevailing culture; this was as true of Greene, as he regarded hell in terms of his own painful early experience, reinforced with literary influences, as it was of the Mexican Indians, mixing Catholicism with native cults and traditions.

Greene spent only about five weeks in Mexico, but it was an extraordinarily fruitful visit. It is, I think, a mistake to treat *The Lawless Roads* simply as a travel book, or even as a collection of source material for *The Power and the Glory*, though episodes and characters from it appear in the novel. It is a work of literary distinction, where Greene employs to the full his capacity for evoking and significantly juxtaposing different levels of reality, whether on a small scale in metaphor, or on a larger scale in the interweaving of narratives. As he was travelling in Mexico, recollections of

London—another of the 'dark places' of the earth in Conrad's phrase—presented themselves as familiar remembered scenes. As I have previously remarked, the advent of radio gave great scope to the Flaubertian juxtaposition, which Greene exploits in virtuoso (and poetic) fashion. He is relaxing in Las Casas at the end of his expedition and one of his companions switches on a short-wave radio broadcast from London:

It was still a Spanish voice speaking in Spanish, but it came from London. It welled out of that solid and complacent building in Portland Place, over the Queen's Hall and Oxford Circus, over the curve of the world, the Atlantic and the Gulf and the Tropic of Capricorn, over the cemetery with 'SILENCIO' in black letters and the wall where Garrido shot his prisoners, over the swamps and rivers, the mountains and the forests, where the old man slept with the rats beside his corn and the flames beat against the front of the locked-up church. 'This is London', they assured me again because I doubted it.

At the end of the book, when he is back in London, Greene encounters familiar scenes with a sense of relief, though as he reflects, 'a bad time over is always tinged with regret'. He missed the extremities of Mexican religion: 'Mass in Chelsea seemed curiously ficti-tious; no peon knelt with his arms out in the attitude of the cross, no woman dragged herself up the aisle on her knees. It would have seemed shocking, like the Agony itself' (ch. 9).

Greene had briefly but favourably reviewed Evelyn Waugh's *Edmund Campion*, and in 1939 Waugh returned the compliment with a longer and admiring review of *The Lawless Roads*. The two men had been nodding acquaintances at Oxford, but they became friends in the 1930s, when they had both converted to Catholicism and made a name as novelists. Waugh wrote, 'Mr Greene is, I think, an Augustinian Christian, a believer of the dark age of Mediterranean decadence when the barbarians were pressing along the frontiers and the City of God seemed yearly more remote and unattainable.'

This may have been true of Greene at that time; it was certainly the way Waugh liked to think of himself. He acknowledges that Greene had good reason to hate Mexico, but ends on the mildly admonitory note that he occasionally directed at his friend (and which Greene never minded): 'The Mexicans are not only the people who killed the martyrs; they are the people for whom the martyrs died.'[1] This point is implicitly present in *The Lawless Roads* and is made explicit in *The Power and the Glory*, which was published in 1940. This is the story of a modern martyr, a Mexican priest who is convinced of his own unworthiness, and whose way of life is indeed very unpriestly, but who, like Fr Pro, and like Fr Campion in the sixteenth century, continues with his mission as best he can, travelling in disguise, saying Mass and hearing confessions, with the forces of the state on his trail. At one point he is thrust into prison for a minor offence but is not recognized—the police have no reliable picture of him—and is released. But he continues his work in danger of his life, which in the end he forfeits. He has crossed into another state where religion is tolerated; he receives a message that a man is dying and needs a priest. He rightly suspects that he has been betrayed, but on a mission of mercy he returns to the area which he has just left. There he is arrested, interrogated, and eventually shot.

In *Ways of Escape* Greene wrote, 'I think *The Power and the Glory* is the only novel I have written to a thesis'; he also remarked, 'The book gave me more satisfaction than any other I had written', which is still probably true of the general response of Greene's readers. *The Power and the Glory* may have been Greene's only novel written to a thesis, but it enacts an imaginative pattern that was already familiar in his fiction: the story of the hunted man. That was the situation of Raven in *A Gun for Sale*, of Hale at the beginning of *Brighton Rock* and later in the novel of Pinkie, his killer, and of D. in *The Confidential Agent*, the 'entertainment' that Greene wrote concurrently with *The Power and the Glory*. The thesis that his

Mexican novel was written to concerns the nature of priesthood. In Catholic doctrine the value of the sacraments is objective and independent of the character of the priest who bestows them, as expressed in the formula *ex opere operato*. The minister must intend to say Mass or administer that sacrament in the appropriate form but his personal character does not affect the efficacy of what he does. Greene's priest is only too aware of his unworthiness. He is a heavy drinker (though probably not a clinical alcoholic, as he is sometimes described) and known as a 'whisky priest'. Though he preserves the practice of celibacy, he has lapsed on one occasion with a woman of his flock and has fathered a daughter. His belief is faltering and he neglects saying the daily prayers of his office, which is hardly surprising given the rigours of his way of life. He could escape to a safer state, where his life would not be in danger, but persists in trying to bring the sacraments to the people.

Like other characters in the first phase of Greene's fiction, the priest is something of an allegorical figure, standing for total dedication to a mission. There is too much we do not know about him for him to emerge as a realistic character. The fabular quality of the narrative is emphasized by the fact that we never learn his name, and two of the other principal figures are also nameless: the mestizo who betrays the priest, a Judas-figure who is one of Greene's menacing grotesques; and the police lieutenant who arrests him, and who embodies a rigorous idealistic atheism. As Greene told Marie-Françoise Allain, 'The *Power and the Glory* was like a seventeenth century play in which the actors symbolize a virtue or a vice, pride, pity, etc. The priest and the lieutenant remained themselves to the end; the priest, for all his recollection of periods in his life when he was different, never changed. The action was contained with a short time-span.'² Greene acknowledged that he had never met a person like the police lieutenant on his travels in Mexico: 'I had to invent him as a counter to the failed priest: the idealistic police officer who stifled life for the best possible motives: the drunken priest who continued to pass life on.' The underlying thesis is evident in *The Power and the Glory*, though the novel develops in a series of memorable scenes. It is full of 'felt life' in its presentation of Mexico, and the physical sensations of the priest. The atmosphere is almost palpably claustrophobic, and much of the action takes place in complete or near darkness. There is the tragiccomic episode when the disguised priest, having with great difficulty obtained wine in order to say Mass, offers some out of politeness to the chief of police, who then proceeds to finish off the bottle. The most powerful episode occurs when the priest, during his temporary imprisonment, is placed in a dark, overcrowded, and stinking cell. A couple are making love in a corner and when a respectable middle-class woman, who has been imprisoned for having religious books in her house, is scandalized, the priest defends them. He discusses life and death with the other prisoners; there is a lot of talk in the novel. After the priest is finally arrested, he and the lieutenant engage in one of the discussions about ultimate values that recur in Greene's novels, from *Stamboul Train* to *The Honorary Consul*; it is in effect a Platonic dialogue between opposing views of the world.

More than any other of Greene's 'Catholic' novels, *The Power and the Glory* makes a direct appeal to non-religious readers. It is a narrative with a simple archetypal power, the story of an isolated man who struggles against all odds to pursue his mission, ultimately at the cost of his life. One critic has written, 'for non-Catholic readers it is precisely the personal, dogged, earth-bound nature of the priest's faith . . . which makes the book credible and sympathetic'.[3] Amongst Catholics the book has been generally admired, though in the 1950s certain Vatican authorities found it objectionable. They complained to the Cardinal Archbishop of Westminster, who passed the word on to Greene: the book was alleged to be 'paradoxical' and dealt with 'extraordinary circumstances', something which might be said of many of the world's greatest novels. Evelyn Waugh was outraged on Greene's behalf, 'Since you showed me the Grand Inquisitor's letter my indignation has waxed. It was as fatuous as unjust—a vile misreading of a noble book.'[4] Greene skilfully finessed the complaint and no more was heard of it. Years later Pope Paul VI, who had read *The Power and the Glory*, told him, 'some parts of your books are certain to offend some Catholics, but you should pay no attention to that.' If there is a doctrinal message in the novel it is that a sinner can become a saint and a martyr. Put in such general terms it is unexceptional, but it emerged from Greene's fascination with the idea that saint and sinner may be very close. A recurring motif in the book comes in the scenes where a respectable Catholic family are clandestinely trying to keep their faith alive. The mother reads to her children out of a life of Fr Pro, which is evidently a work of sanitized hagiography; *The Power and the Glory* might be described as an anti-hagiography, though the final scene, when a new priest arrives to take over the dead man's work, is more like the orthodox variety.

The Vatican readers might have had more specific reasons for their objections than the priest's lack of the superficial signs of sanctity. In his dialogue with the police lieutenant he defends himself:

'Listen,' the priest said earnestly, leaning forward in the dark, pressing on a cramped foot. 'I'm not as dishonest as you think I am. Why do you think I tell people out of the pulpit that they're in danger of damnation if death catches them unawares? I'm not telling them fairy stories I don't believe myself. I don't know a thing about the mercy of God: I don't know how awful the human heart looks to Him. But I do know this—that if there's ever been a single man in this state damned, then I'll be damned too.' He said slowly, 'I wouldn't want it to be any different. I just want justice, that's all.'

Greene is recalling Péguy's idea of solidarity with the damned, which he had touched on in *Brighton Rock* and *The Lawless Roads*. The priest's words can be interpreted in different ways, but on the face of it he seems to want a justice that is different from, perhaps higher than, God's justice. This is indeed paradoxical; and so, I think, are some of the things the priest says when he is preaching at a clandestine Mass, which might have puzzled his simple listeners. As so often in Greene's Catholic writings, the fear of Hell looms larger than the hope of Heaven, and a loving God is not often talked about. When he is about to be executed the priest finds he has no fear of damnation, only an immense sense of disappointment, as he has to go to God with nothing achieved: 'It seemed to him at that moment, that it would have been quite easy to be a saint. It would only have needed a little self-restraint and a little courage. He felt like someone who has missed happiness by seconds at an appointed place. He knew now that at the end there was only one thing that counted—to be a saint.' But the informed reader knows that the priest has achieved sanctity, by the time-honoured path of martyrdom. *The Power and the Glory* takes Greene's preoccupation with the relation between sinner and saint, first evident in his discussion of Frederick Rolfe, almost as far as it can go. But he had not yet finished with the topic.

The Power and the Glory deserves its high reputation.* It is a powerful book, but it achieves its power because of its narrowness, like a jet of water under pressure. Greene's earlier novels had, for the most part, English settings; in *Stamboul Train* a group of English people are transported by train across Europe, while in *England Made Me*, after some after evocative accounts of London, the story moves to Sweden. But Sweden does not seem all that different from

---

* In *Graham Greene: Friend and Brother*, Fr Leopoldo Durán writes that Greene had been reading Bernard Bergonzi's book about him. The present work is the first such book I have written and the reference is evidently to my *Reading the Thirties*, which discusses early Greene. He is reported to have appreciated the complimentary references, but complained that I was too dismissive of *The Power and the Glory*. I now think he was right; I failed to do justice to that book and am happy to set the record straight.

England, and most of the characters are English. As Greene told
Julian Maclaren-Ross in 1938, he felt that England, and London in
particular, was his natural territory as a writer. In *The Power and the
Glory* he moves far away from it. He constructs Mexico from the
notes he made on his five-week trip and from intensely detailed
memories; one of the strangest things Greene ever wrote about
himself was his remark in *In Search of a Character*, 'I have very little
visual imagination and only a short memory.' In fact, the novel is
full of visually compelling scenes, from the opening sentence
onward: 'Mr Trench went out to look for his ether cylinder, in the
blazing Mexican sun and the bleaching dust. A few vultures looked
down from the roof with shabby indifference; he wasn't carrion
yet.' At the same time, as Greene remarked in *The Lawless Roads*,
'Mexico is a state of mind'. When he was writing about England his
subject matter was all around him; now he had to retrieve it from
notes and memories. Hence the narrowness, at least of the novel; in
The Lawless Roads Greene plays off memories of England against
the realities of Mexico.

The novel is about a Mexican in his native land, from which we
cannot move away, presenting a sense of claustrophobic confine-
ment. Linguistically, too, the novel is confined. Most of the conversations are supposed to be in Spanish, though the priest is said to
know English, having studied in the United States, and sometimes
uses it when talking to foreigners. Greene does a better job of
putting Spanish into English than Hemingway did in *For Whom the
Bell Tolls*, but he has to use a plain style, which gives no scope to his
good ear for contemporary English speech and idioms. And in an
irritating Hollywood touch, he inserts occasional words in Spanish.
He restrains the complex metaphors that occurred in his previous
fiction, but engages in some arresting but inert similes: 'he could
feel his prayers weigh him down like undigested food'; 'he drank
the brandy down like damnation'; 'Evil ran like malaria in his veins'.

W. H. Auden was given to such yokings of the concrete and the abstract, and Greene, who admired him, may have been prompted to imitate them.* Given that Greene had abandoned so many of the resources of his fiction, it is remarkable that *The Power and the Glory* works as well as it does. But when one thinks of the way in which *Brighton Rock* combines and contrasts different levels of reality, the homogeneous but confined narrative of *The Power and the Glory* appears a lesser though still substantial achievement.

NOTES

1. Evelyn Waugh, *Essays, Articles and Reviews*, ed. Donat Gallagher (London, 1983), 249–50.
2. M. -F. Allain, *The Other Man* (Harmondsworth, 1984), 136.
3. John Spurling, *Graham Greene* (London, 1983), 36.
4. Evelyn Waugh, *Letters*, ed. Mark Amory (Harmondsworth, 1982), 422.

* See 'Auden and the Audenesque' in my *Reading the Thirties* (London, 1978).

6

A Catholic Novelist?

IN 1948 Greene published *The Heart of the Matter*. It was his first novel for five years, and quickly became a best-seller on both sides of the Atlantic, placing him among the leading English novelists of his generation. It was of particular interest to Catholic readers and provoked much debate among them; following *Brighton Rock* and *The Power and the Glory*, Greene came to be regarded as a prominent Catholic novelist, though it was a description he disliked and resisted, preferring to think of himself as a Catholic who happened to write novels. Evident themes relate *The Heart of the Matter* to the two previous 'Catholic' novels, so much so that some critics have seen it as the conclusion of a kind of trilogy. It is true that the central characters of all three—Pinkie, the whisky priest, and Major Scobie, the colonial police officer—have things in common. Each is desperately isolated, a Catholic who is in a state of mortal sin, or fears he may be, and who is ready to consider damnation as an alternative to salvation. But despite these affinities, *The Heart of the Matter* represents a new stage in Greene's literary career.

In his conversations with Allain, Greene claimed that religious conviction meant that a writer's characters had greater depth and power than those of an unbeliever: 'I think that the flatness of E. M. Forster's characters, and Virginia Woolf's or Sartre's, for example, compared with the astonishing vitality of Bloom in Joyce's *Ulysses*, or of Balzac's *Père Goriot*, or of David Copperfield, derives from the absence of the religious dimension in the former.'[1] The claim is not convincing as it stands. Balzac and Dickens may have kept up a formal commitment to their respective Catholicism and Protestantism, but Joyce, when he created Bloom, was no longer a believer, even though his imagination had been deeply affected by his Jesuit education. George Eliot, the inventor of Mr Casaubon and Gwendolyn Harleth, was an unbeliever (albeit a devout one), as were other great creators of fictional character. It is an interesting argument, which I shall not pursue here; I merely want to pick up Greene's remark about the 'astonishing vitality' of David Copperfield; David is indeed a solidly established character with the capacity to change and learn and grow that we look for in the hero of the realistic *Bildungsroman*. But there is a much greater vitality in Mr Micawber and Uriah Heep and Betsey Trottwood and the other memorable grotesques and caricatures who populate the novel; they, after all, are what we call essentially 'Dickensian'. As I have suggested, in his earlier career Greene wrote a kind of fiction that had affinities with Dickens's, where the caricatures or the archetypal figures were more convincing than the attempts at realistic character-drawing. In *The Heart of the Matter*, though, he presents a central figure of a conventional kind, with a degree of psychological depth and complexity.

Henry Scobie is a police officer, a type whom Greene had presented in previous works as admirable examples of unimaginative integrity, like the Assistant Commissioner in *It's a Battlefield* and Mather in *A Gun for Sale* (and *mutatis mutandis* the police lieutenant in *The Power and the Glory*). Scobie has served for many years in a British colony in West Africa (unnamed, but based on Sierra Leone, where Greene was an intelligence officer in 1942–3). He is middle-aged, a Catholic convert married to a discontented, nagging Catholic wife, Louise, whom he no longer loves, if he ever did. Their only child had died some years before. His career is in the doldrums and Louise is deeply distressed when Scobie does not get the promotion he had been hoping for. But he remains attached to the colony, hot and uncomfortable though it is. Greene lays on thick local colour, in the way of sights, sounds, smells, and other physical sensations. He had done as much in writing about Mexico, but there he had been restricted to the notes he had made and the memories he retained after a visit of only five weeks; *The Power and the Glory* is a narrative without any margins of experience to draw on, whereas Greene lived in Sierra Leone for a year and was saturated in the life of the place, as he showed to good effect. Whereas he had hated Mexico, Greene retained a certain affection for West Africa. He confessed that when he returned to novel-writing after a long gap his technical skills were rusty and he felt uncertain about relating his characters and managing the transitions between scenes. I think this shows in *The Heart of the Matter*; one sign of authorial uncertainty may be the excessively elaborate organization of a fairly short novel: it is divided into books, parts, and chapters, with numbered subdivisions within the chapters. It is as though Greene felt he could not sustain the scenic method without these formal props. Unlike his previous fiction, *The Heart of the Matter* lacks a poetic dimension, despite a scatter of rather mechanical similes. But there is some good writing in it. I am not thinking of the examination of Scobie's emotional and spiritual tangles, but of the extended description, which occupies chapter 1 of Book Two, of the arrival of a party of survivors from a torpedoed ship who had spent forty days in an open boat. They include two children, one of whom dies soon after arrival, and the 19-year-old widow Helen Rolt, who will fatally complicate Scobie's life. This is a compelling episode, closer to empathetic journalism than to Greene's other fictional modes, and offers, in anticipation, some warrant for Zadie Smith's description of him as a great journalist.

The figures in the foreground, though, Scobie, Louise, and the other members of the expatriate British community, are a rather dull lot. I use that adjective with a sense of its various associations: artistic, social, moral, and psychological. Though I miss the grotesques and humours of the earlier novels, there are a few of these outside the ranks of the English community, notably the monstrous Syrian trader Yusuf who ensnares Scobie: he is a corrupt and fascinating figure, in the line of Minty and Cholmondeley alias Davis, or, indeed, Pinkie. But the heart of Greene's matter is the sad story of Major Scobie. He is a good man, of conspicuous integrity and devoted to his job, but he starts making mistakes, and one leads to another. He breaks regulations to save the career of the captain of a Portuguese ship, who has appealed to him on the basis of their shared Catholicism. He borrows money from Yusuf, legally but imprudently, in order to send Louise on a long holiday in South Africa when she needs to get away from him for a while. During her absence he embarks on an affair—certainly one of the most lugubrious adulteries in fiction—with Helen Rolt. Worse follows. When Yusuf starts blackmailing him, Scobie helps him to smuggle diamonds out of the colony. Then Scobie's devoted servant Ali is murdered in ambiguous circumstances, probably on Yusuf's orders, and Scobie feels appropriately guilty. Finally, after his wife has returned from South Africa, he agrees to join her in receiving Holy Communion; a sacrilegious act, as he has not been shriven for the mortal sin of adultery and is indeed continuing his affair with Helen. Scobie feels sorry for Louise and for Helen, and then starts feeling sorry for God. He resolves to get himself out of an intolerable situation, and he commits suicide; he tries to make it look like death from natural causes, but the truth emerges. He has committed what many Catholics at that time regarded as the ultimate sin, one which, in the nature of the act, cannot be forgiven. Greene's preoccupation with suicide is evident in his autobiographical writings, and it was a motif in his fiction and drama from *The Man Within* onwards. That novel ends with the two protagonists taking their lives; earlier in *The Heart of the Matter* Scobie has to deal with the case of Pemberton, a young district commissioner in a remote outpost, who has hanged himself.

'Is Scobie damned?' was a question for urgent debate among Catholics, though some of them felt the situation was implausible and factitious. Greene's friend Tom Burns, a Catholic publisher who had commissioned his book on Mexico, and later became editor of *The Tablet*, wrote of *The Heart of the Matter* in harsh terms:

G.G. uses all the apparatus of the Catechism & bad sermons twanging away on an exhausted id & irritated nerves to produce a sham spiritual drama: a caricature conventional Catholic couple is very cruelly trotted out to cut capers in the world of apprehensions much more the novelist's than their own. He almost turns things upside down & hates the sinners while he loves the sin. G.G. is becoming a sort of smart-Alec of Jansenism.[2]

Burns's point about 'bad sermons' is well taken. Scobie is about to participate in a sacrilegious Communion, which is likely to be followed by others as long as he keeps up the deception: 'He had a sudden picture before his eyes of a bleeding face, of eyes closed by the continuous shower of blows: the punch-drunk head of God reeling sideways.' In this extraordinary image Scobie draws on extravagant and decadent modes of pulpit rhetoric and religious art. As the narrative unfolds his religious thinking becomes increasingly far-out, eventually coming to the conclusion that Christ's death on the cross was a form of suicide: 'Christ had not been murdered: you couldn't murder God: he had hung himself on the cross as surely as Pemberton from the picture rail.'

Evelyn Waugh's response to the novel was more circumspect than Burns's. Since publishing *Brideshead Revisited* in 1945 he too had been widely identified as a Catholic novelist, and unlike Greene he was happy with that description. Indeed, he thought of Greene and himself as partners in an important enterprise, the modern English

Catholic novel, who should be mutually supportive. In his review he notes how *The Heart of the Matter* continues the interest in damnation first expressed in *Brighton Rock*, and writes uncompromisingly, 'It is a book which only a Catholic could write and only a Catholic could understand. I mean that only a Catholic could understand the nature of the problem.' Waugh fears that the book's wide sale, particularly in America, means it will have many readers who do not understand it. He also fears that many loyal Catholics will be put off this 'profoundly reverent book' because of its scandalous material and because it does not make glowing propaganda for the Church. Waugh takes the book very seriously and discusses it in detail; but despite the respectful tone it is evident that he does not like it very much. He gives a careful account of all the ways in which Scobie goes wrong until he finally accepts damnation as the only way out, and concludes, 'To me the idea of willing my own damnation for the love of God is either a very loose poetical expression or a mad blasphemy, for the God who accepted that sacrifice could neither be just nor lovable.' Waugh also takes issue with the epigraph from Péguy which asserts that the sinner is at the heart of Christianity; Waugh has taken the trouble to read the essay from which the quotation comes and subjects it to a withering analysis (though the quotation itself could be read as a gloss on Christ's words in Matthew 9: 12, 'They that be whole need not a physician but they that are sick'). He concludes his review, 'Mr Greene has removed the argument from Péguy's mumbled version and restated it in brilliantly plain human terms; and it is there, at the heart of the matter, that the literary critic must resign his judgment to the theologian.'[3]

Waugh's final point was in fact taken up by a theologian, Canon Joseph Cartmell, in a postscript to the review. He agrees with Waugh's judgement, and says that Scobie's faith becomes a dead faith, since it is without charity, and he is 'a very bad moral coward'.

Cartmell's concluding comments show the theologian to be also a good literary critic:

The study of Scobie is done with power. But I feel a weakness. No man can indeed appreciate to the full the idea of the eternal loss of God; but here one is left with the impression that Scobie is merely going into exile in the next world; in his heart he regrets to lose God, but, since he was always happiest when alone, he will not, in the long run, when he has got used to things in the beyond, be very unhappy; he will have the peace of the solitary. Briefly, in spite of his shrinking, he takes Hell very quietly.[4]

Pinkie had had no doubts about the traditional Hell: 'Of course there's Hell. Flames and damnation.' But Scobie is more cautious, as we see from a dinner-table conversation:

'But do you really, seriously, Major Scobie,' Dr Sykes asked, 'believe in Hell?'

'Oh yes I do.'

'In flames and torment?'

'Perhaps not quite that. They tell us it may be a permanent sense of loss.'

'That sort of Hell wouldn't worry *me*,' Fellowes said.

'Perhaps you've never lost anything of importance', Scobie said. (part 3, ch. 2, 1)

(For the characters in a later novel about Catholics, David Lodge's *How Far Can You Go?*, published in 1980, Hell suddenly disappears at some point in the 1960s.)

James Wood has given an acute account of Greene's problems in presenting Scobie:

Scobie has not enough depth as a character to convince us of his self-divisions. It may be that in order for a character to seem self-divided, we must feel the weight both of his composed self and the weight, as it were, of his discomposed halves. Scobie, by contrast, is only monochromatically vivid. He is that knowable type, 'a policeman', and has the temperament familiar to us now from a thousand television shows: work-obsessed, calm, controlling, repressed, bad with women, a grim solitary. He seems to have had almost no childhood, and to have no interests outside his work. Or rather he has one great passion other than his work, and it is religion; but it is a passion that does not emerge as such until it is negatively provoked. (He feels, oddly, religious pain but no religious joy.)[5]

Greene himself was one of the sharpest critics of the novel, which he regarded as a failure. He wrote in *Ways of Escape*:

The scales to me seem too heavily weighted, the plot overloaded, the religious scruples of Scobie too extreme. I had meant the story of Scobie to enlarge a theme which I had touched on in *The Ministry of Fear*, the disastrous effect on human beings of pity as distinct from compassion. I had written in *The Ministry of Fear*: 'Pity is cruel. Pity destroys. Love isn't safe when pity's prowling around.' The character of Scobie was intended to show that pity can be the expression of an almost monstrous pride. But I found the effect on readers was quite different. To them Scobie was exonerated, Scobie was a 'good man', he was hunted to his doom by the harshness of his wife . . . Suicide was Scobie's inevitable end; the particular motive of his suicide, to save even God from himself, was the final twist of the screw of his inordinate pride. Perhaps Scobie should have been a subject for a cruel comedy rather than for tragedy. (ch. 4, 2)

Greene's analysis is sound but it was written after the event; if readers were misguided enough to sympathize and identify with Scobie it was because the narrative encouraged them to; he is presented without detachment or distance. Conor Cruise O'Brien refers, in a good phrase, to 'a constant hum of approbation for Scobie himself'.[6] (The essays by O'Brien and Wood, written more than fifty years apart, contain some of the best criticism of *The Heart of the Matter* that I know.) Greene's throwaway remark that Scobie could have been the subject for a cruel comedy is at first glance startling, but I can see what he is getting at; in a different perspective Scobie could appear as a ludicrously blundering incompetent, a Mr Magoo of the moral life. This may have been what Greene wanted but it is not, in the writing, what he actually did. Discussing the character of Rose in *Brighton Rock*, I remarked that it would have taken

Dostoevsky to have described her as fully as she deserved. And one might say something similar about Scobie, that tragic-comic figure, consumed by pity and pride and yet so humble and unassuming, so evidently a good man and good at his work, who nevertheless goes around doing harm.

The End of the Affair is the last of Greene's novels to reflect an overtly Catholic set of values. But unlike the 'trilogy' of 1938–48, the emphasis is not on mortal sin, Hell, and damnation, features which have their own melodramatic appeal to the unbelieving reader, but on sanctity and God's intervention in human affairs and the possibility of miracles. In Ian Gregor's words, 'The theme is, quite simply, grace.'[7] Though the novel was well received, these topics were harder for a lay audience to accept. *The End of the Affair* is one of Greene's best novels, and it is unlike anything else he wrote. There are obvious formal innovations, as Greene discusses in *Ways of Escape*. One of them is first-person narration, 'that damned autobiographical form,' as Henry James disparagingly called it. Greene had already employed it for the novella he had written as the basis for the film of *The Third Man* (published in 1950), though in the loose and cheating form in which the narrator describes scenes at which he was not present (something that Greene complained about in Proust). The novella, which Greene describes as no more than 'the raw material for a picture', was the foundation for a classic film, in which Greene's close collaboration with the director Carol Reed produced memorably poetic effects. In *The End of the Affair* he follows the first-person convention properly, having, as he says, been captivated by the apparent ease with which Dickens used it in *David Copperfield*, though in practice Greene found it difficult to manage. In his previous novels he had brought in a multiplicity of narrative voices or points of view; even central presences like the whisky priest or Scobie do not see or experience everything that goes on in the story. But in *The End of the Affair* there are only two

voices: that of the narrator, Maurice Bendrix, and of his lover Sarah
Miles, as it rises from her purloined journal. Again, the fluidity of the
time-scheme, which moves back and forth between 1939 and 1946,
following the uncertain course of memory, is something new in
Greene. He acknowledges that in this aspect he had learnt from a
novel he greatly admired and frequently returned to, Ford Madox
Ford's *The Good Soldier*, which also makes ingenious use of first-person narrative. Greene told Marie-Françoise Allain that his prose had
become simpler with *The End of the Affair*; he saw this development
as marking a break with features of his earlier writing which he
repudiated, extravagant metaphors and 'poetic prose'. It is part of
my argument that in Greene plainer is not necessarily better; in fact,
there are some compelling metaphors in *The End of the Affair*, which
emerge the more strikingly from the plain background; for instance,
'the telephone presented nothing but the silent open mouth of
somebody found dead'.

The End of the Affair is the story of a triangle: the love affair
between Maurice Bendrix, a novelist, and Sarah Miles, the wife of an
amiable but dim civil servant, Henry Miles. It goes on for several
years during the Second World War. There are a few other characters who play subsidiary but necessary roles. And in the end, another
character intervenes to destroy the triangle: God. During a flying
bomb attack on London in 1944 Maurice and Sarah are in a house
which is badly damaged. She sees her lover lying under a door that
has been blown off its hinges and is convinced that he is dead. Then,
although she has never previously professed any religious beliefs,
she kneels and prays to God to restore him to life, saying that if that
happens she will give him up. In fact, Maurice is only stunned and
soon extricates himself. (There were similar episodes in bombed
houses in *The Confidential Agent* and *The Ministry of Fear*.) In the rest
of the story Sarah is trying to keep her promise, even though she still
loves him, and Maurice is trying to get her back. She feels the pull of

the God in whom she has never particularly believed, and starts taking instruction in the Catholic faith. At the end of the novel she is dead and Maurice and Henry have become friends. Maurice fears that God, having taken Sarah from him, is now turning to him. In the last words of the novel, he begs God to leave him alone: 'You've robbed me of enough, I'm too tired and old to learn to love, leave me alone for ever.' Bendrix fights to retain his atheism, but the single word, 'then', in the opening paragraph suggests he is not successful: 'if I had believed then in a God . . .'

In all of Greene's previous novels there had been a social and material background presented in detail, whether it was London or Brighton, Mexico or West Africa. But in *The End of the Affair* the attention is concentrated on the two central figures, and the setting is merely sketched in. Although the story unfolds in London over several years, there are no evocative panoramas of the capital, not even any strong indication of a city at war. The flying bomb that precipitates the crisis between the lovers is merely a plot device, in contrast to the phantasmagoric rendering of the Blitz in *The Ministry of Fear*. Roger Sharrock has given a perceptive account of the way in which the narrative is concentrated. He remarks that until the death of Sarah towards the end of the book:

the ostensible subject is an illicit love affair. It is a natural history of love concentrating on the psychology of passion in a manner that is more French than English . . . his trio of protagonists are isolated and if Henry has a slightly comic external life of Whitehall committees and the expectation of honours it only emphasises his separation from the intense life of the lovers. Greene too depicts the love affair as endowed with the vitality of an organism and Bendrix, with his intense jealousy, fears and anticipates the death of love.[8]

Sharrock sees *The End of the Affair* as more like a French novel than an English one; one recalls that *The Good Soldier*, the novel that influenced it and is subtitled 'A Tale of Passion', was once described as 'the best French novel in English'. There are passages where Greene—or Bendrix—seems to speak in the sententious tones of a French moralist: 'The words of human love have been used by the saints to describe their vision of God, and so, I suppose, we might use the terms of prayer, meditation, contemplation to explain the intensity of the love we feel for a woman.'

It is generally known that Maurice and Sarah are closely drawn from Greene himself and Catherine Walston, his lover for several years, to whom the novel was dedicated. Whatever the human interest of this knowledge, which is made much of by readers drawn to biography rather than criticism, it is not relevant to the quality of the book. It is not difficult to sense the personal pressure driving Bendrix on in his obsessive career, but the association of author and character is not in itself a guarantee of a convincing fictional creation. Whatever his origins in Greene's psyche and experience, Bendrix emerges from the page as a convincing character of great power who defines himself in his own words. Similarly, Sarah has depth and credibility, whatever her origins; she is Greene's most successful female character (as opposed to types or caricatures, which were appropriate in the different conventions governing the early novels). One can concede, though, that Bendrix is a very Greeneian writer, and so indeed is Sarah in her journal, even down to the occasional metaphor: 'Why did this promise stay, like an ugly vase a friend has given and one waits for the maid to break it and year after year she breaks the things one values and the ugly vase remains?'

Jealousy arises from the deadly combination of love and hate, and Bendrix is a good hater. He hates Henry for possessing Sarah, he hates her when she is trying to end the affair, he hates the unknown lover who he thinks has enticed her away, and when he discovers it is not a lover but God, then he hates God. And throughout the story he hates himself. Lodge has noted of *The End of the*

Affair, 'it rings with the repetition of *love* and *hate*. For the statistical record, these words or forms of them recur about three hundred and one hundred times respectively in this short novel.'[9] Bendrix powerfully reveals his own negation, establishing himself as a presence of what Frank Kermode has called 'vicious energy'.[10] There are not many parallels in fiction; John Dowell in *The Good Soldier* is a weak and deluded man, whereas Bendrix is domineering and unscrupulously manipulative. Greene may, though, have been influenced by François Mauriac's *Knot of Vipers*, which he had read before the war and been impressed by. It is narrated by Louis, an elderly *rentier* who is nearing the end of his life and is consumed by schemes for revenging himself on his family. Both narrators refer to their hatred on the first page of the novel; in the background of both I sense the possible presence of Dostoevsky's Underground Man, eloquently spewing out his bitterness and resentment against humanity and the world. The intensity of Bendrix's narrative carries one along so effectively that one passes over weaknesses in the plot, notably the way in which he acquires Sarah's journal. It is taken by Mr Parkiss, the shabby-genteel private detective whom Bendrix has employed to spy on Sarah (a Dickensian figure and one of Greene's most likeable characters). He gets hold of it by befriending her maid and thereby being admitted to the house: an implausible device reminiscent of old-fashioned detective novels. He steals the journal without any difficulty, but, as Evelyn Waugh asked in an enthusiastic review of *The End of the Affair*, wouldn't it have been missed?

Though *The End of the Affair* is narrated by a novelist, it is not a novel about writing a novel in the Sternean manner. But Bendrix frequently refers to the problems of storytelling; the book's first words are, 'A story has no beginning and no end: arbitrarily one chooses that moment of experience from which to look back or from which to look ahead.' Near the end of the novel Bendrix pays reluctant tribute to God as a superior novelist. He reflects how in the course of writing some characters remain inert, refuse to come alive, but they are still necessary to the story:

I can imagine a God feeling in just that way about some of us. The saints, one would suppose, in a sense create themselves. They come alive. They are capable of the surprising act or word. They stand outside the plot, unconditioned by it. But we have to be pushed around. We have the obstinacy of non-existence. We are inextricably bound to the plot, and wearily God forces us, here and there, according to his intention, characters without poetry, without free will, whose only importance is somewhere, at some time, we help to furnish the scene in which a living character moves and speaks, providing perhaps the saints with the opportunities for *their* free will. (book 4, 8)

It would be possible for a non-believer to appreciate *The End of the Affair* as a distinguished work of fiction, and indeed many such readers have. One could read it as a psychological study in obsession and delusion on the part of both Maurice and Sarah, without accepting the reality of the cause of the delusions. But the miracles remain a stumbling block. Mr Parkiss, has a young son whom Sarah once briefly met and was kind to. The boy falls very ill with appendicitis, and claims that in a dream Sarah appeared to him after her death. Soon after this he makes an astonishingly rapid recovery. Mr Parkiss tells Bendrix that he had been praying hard for his son; to God, to his late wife who he was sure was in heaven; and to Sarah, whom he is starting to regard as a saint. It is not specifically claimed that the boy's recovery is a miracle—such instant recoveries could happen in the natural order—but there is a suggestion of divine intervention about it. The case of Richard Smythe is more of a challenge. He is a crusading atheist, a soap-box orator who preaches against religion on Clapham Common. He is a handsome man whose face, in the original edition of *The End of the Affair*, is badly disfigured by a strawberry birthmark. Sarah consults him in an effort to suppress her stirrings towards religious belief, but his arguments have the opposite effect.

Meanwhile, Smythe falls in love with her. After her death he confesses to Bendrix that his birthmark has disappeared. In physiological terms this is an impossible event, a tougher proposition than the young boy's sudden cure from a severe illness. It would have a good claim to be classed as a miracle by the Catholic Church's criteria for assessing such phenomena. Secular readers were unhappy about both the likelihood of these events and what they were trying to imply in the narrative. And so, in time, was Greene. In later editions he tampered with the text, so that the strawberry birthmark that Sarah noticed when she first saw him has become 'gross livid spots', a less specific disfigurement and one whose later disappearance need not be regarded as a miracle if one prefers a natural explanation. Greene should not have bothered; the change is not an improvement, and the story continues to suggest that the adulterous Sarah has become a saint in heaven; the last and most startling example in Greene's fiction of the interchangeability of sinner and saint.

Evelyn Waugh welcomed the miracles. His admiring review of The End of the Affair showed he was happier with it than with The Heart of the Matter. He noted the ways in which it represented a new start in Greene's career both as a novelist and as a Catholic writer. Waugh remarks, 'there is active beneficent supernatural interference. This is a brave invention of Mr Greene's. His voice is listened to in many dark places and this defiant assertion of the supernatural is entirely admirable.' Waugh himself had hinted at the sudden descent of grace when, in Brideshead Revisited, he presented the deathbed repentance of the defiant apostate Lord Marchmain. But his friend had been bolder in describing actual miracles, or perhaps a miracle and a half. Waugh touches on another weakness in The End of the Affair. After Sarah's death her mother reveals that when Sarah was a small child she had had her baptized as a Catholic, by a local priest when they were on holiday in France, in a sudden impulse to spite her husband. Thereafter Sarah had no more contact with Catholicism, but the implication is that the grace implanted in her secret baptism fructifies into faith after a worldly and adulterous life. The whole situation is unconvincing; I very much doubt if a priest would have agreed (or been empowered) to carry out a clandestine baptism on someone who was not in danger of death. Waugh remarks, 'There is some speculation as to whether it "took"; whether it was an infection caught in infancy, and so on. But Mr Greene knows very well that she would have been as surely baptized by the local vicar.' Waugh's last comment blurs a necessary distinction. In Catholic doctrine baptism by any Christian minister (or a layperson in case of emergency) validly admits one into the larger Christian community. But Catholic baptism means that the person receiving it is henceforth a Catholic, and however much they fall away they can reassume sacramental life without further formality once they have repented. The rest of Waugh's comment is valid and important; he puts his finger on Greene's tendency to regard sacramental action as a vaccination or an infection, or a magic spell. He gives his friend a kindly warning, 'I can imagine some passages carrying a whiff of occultism.'[11] References in the text support Waugh's point. Sarah writes in her last letter to Bendrix, 'I've caught belief like a disease'; after her death and the revelation about her growing attachment to Catholicism, Henry says, 'Baptized at two years old and then beginning to go back to what you can't even remember . . . It's like an infection.' Sarah's readiness to see herself as a victim of divine infection points to a certain passivity in her temperament, which Ian Gregor discusses in his acute and demandingly subtle essay on the novel; he observes, 'We can see that a result of Sarah's "life in the moment" is that any form of moral appraisal is rendered null and void; an act is simply what it is, having neither history nor consequence.'

At the beginning of his essay Gregor refers to the problems raised by the Catholic dimension of *The End of the Affair*, whether the readers are believers or not. He distinguishes 'between theology and theology-in-fiction, between "views" and "the use of views" as artistic material'. It is an essential distinction and one which I have tried to preserve in this study. The novel has had an interesting range of critical responses, from both Catholics and non-Catholics. Amongst the latter, Frank Kermode has referred to it as 'almost beyond question Mr Greene's masterpiece, his fullest and most completely realized book', though he acknowledges that 'the unwilling sanctification of Sarah' presents difficulties.[12] In the same category, Michael Gorra, in his introduction to the American Penguin edition of 2004, whilst admiring much of the book, baulks at the miracles: 'those last chapters are enough to keep one from fully sharing Kermode's judgment. They cheapen the experience this novel describes'. Amongst Catholics, Evelyn Waugh, despite some minor reservations, thought highly of *The End of the Affair*, particularly the miracles. Ian Gregor was a Catholic and a qualified admirer of the book, but he rejected the idea of Sarah's sanctification. In my own view the miracles are a difficulty in the plausibility of the narrative, and any attempt to justify them, as Waugh did, is likely to move from theology-in-fiction to theology itself. And Greene's later tampering with the narrative was a mistake. I agree with Kermode that the novel was one of Greene's finest achievements in fiction, whilst not quite seeing it as his masterpiece, a position I reserve for *Brighton Rock*. I have to acknowledge that it does not easily fit into my approach in this study, which follows Allott and Ferris in seeing early Greene as a dramatic poet rather than a conventional novelist, closer to Webster than to Thackeray or Trollope. This does not apply to *The End of the Affair*, which is sparing with poetic devices and rhetoric and is a work of concentrated psychological realism. It may not recall the great Victorians, but it has French affinities, particularly with François Mauriac. If Greene had written more novels like *The End of the Affair* my argument could not have been sustained. But it remains a remarkable, unique achievement, at a level which Greene never reached again.

Greene's possible debt to Mauriac is uncertain. In his conversations with Marie-Françoise Allain he said that he was a great admirer of some of Mauriac's books, but thought that the French novelist's intense loyalty to Catholicism made him too 'scrupulous' a writer, in a theological rather than a moral sense. He told her that the first book by Mauriac that he encountered was *A Knot of Vipers*, which he read in the 1930s. As I have suggested, Greene may have got from this novel the idea of a first-person narrator with strong negative characteristics. Elsewhere in Mauriac's oeuvre there are motifs that recall Greene; as for instance in *The Desert of Love*, when Dr Courrèges says of the *femme fatale* Maria Cross, 'I know what Maria Cross has been through, and I know that somewhere in her there are the makings of a saint'. In Mauriac's *The Enemy* (*Le Mal*) another free-living woman, Fanny Barrett, attacks the rigorously Catholic Madam Dézaymeries for turning her out of the house when she learns that Fanny has been divorced and remarried: 'How I hate this religion of yours for coming between us. I would hate Him for coming between us—if he existed!' This is close to one of Bendrix's tirades; the final words of *The Enemy* seem to point to *The End of the Affair*: 'Where is the artist who may dare to imagine the shifts and processes of the great protagonist—Grace?' Greene's only piece of writing about Mauriac is a short essay that appeared in 1945 in a French newspaper published in London and was subsequently included in his *Collected Essays*. He sets out the argument that he later expanded to Allain, that in a secular world the characters of novels were diminished as human beings: 'with the death of James the religious sense was lost to the English novel, and with the religious sense went the sense of the importance of the human act.' Greene finds this religious sense and a corresponding depth of representation in the novels of

Mauriac, and he goes on to discuss *La Pharisienne* in admiring tones, invoking both Shakespeare and Pascal. But when he was interviewed by Martin Shuttleworth and Simon Raven in 1953, he played down any possible interest he had in Mauriac: 'I read *Thérèse* in 1930 and was turned up inside but, as I have said, I don't think he had any influence on me unless it was an unconscious one.'[13] Greene gives a different account of his first acquaintance with Mauriac from the one he later gave Allain, but that can be put down to the vagaries of memory. More interestingly, the interviewers are wrong when they claim that Greene had once acknowledged Mauriac's influence. Allott and Ferris write, 'Greene acknowledges that the attempt to deal with Catholic themes in his novels is owed to the reading of Mauriac', [14] and give as their source the exchange of letters between Greene, Elizabeth Bowen, and V. S. Pritchett published in 1948 as *Why Do I Write?* But in that collection Greene's only reference to Mauriac is to his personal apologia for his career as a Catholic novelist: 'If my conscience were as acute as M. Mauriac's showed itself to be in his essay, *God and Mammon*, I could not write a line.' Error has been added to Greene's habitual indirection to produce confusion.

Nevertheless, whenever Greene started reading Mauriac, by the mid-1940s, at the time he published his essay on him, Greene was becoming very familiar with Mauriac's fiction. There were professional reasons for this. He had become a director of the publishing house of Eyre and Spottiswood and in that capacity commissioned a series of translations of Mauriac's books by Gerard Hopkins, which appeared between 1946 and 1958; the process of seeing them through the press would have given him an intimate acquaintance with at least the earlier titles, such as *Thérèse* and *La Pharisienne*, which appeared before he left the company. It is possible that this renewed acquaintance with Mauriac suggested ways of writing a new kind of novel, which combined psychological realism with religious depths. Greene thought that *The End of the Affair* should have been longer. He wrote in *Ways of Escape*,

Sarah, the chief character was dead, the book should have continued at least as long after her death as before, and yet, like her lover Bendrix, I found I had no great appetite to continue once she was dead and only a philosophical theme was left behind . . . The coincidences should have continued over the years, battering the mind of Bendrix, forcing on him a reluctant doubt of his own atheism.

Such extended analysis of the progress of a strong but negative character was the kind of thing that Mauriac did well, as in the presentation of Joseph in *Knot of Vipers*, of Brigitte Pian in *A Woman of the Pharisees*, and Thérèse Desqueyroux, carried through two novels and some short stories. In *God and Mammon* Mauriac referred to his tendency to Jansenism, the mode of rigorous, joyless, and puritanical Catholicism that emerged in seventeenth-century France, and whose most famous adherent was Pascal. It is a spirit that permeates Mauriac's novels, whose characters are neurotically scrupulous and self-tormenting. It is in striking contrast to the cheerful, unreflective quality of Italian Catholicism, for instance. The lesson is that religion is never apprehended in a pure state, but is always affected, and often distorted, by contingent cultural and temperamental elements. Greene was sometimes described as 'Jansenist' by critics of his Catholic novels. In that context it is at best a very loose term, given how remote he was from the French culture in which it was rooted, but it can be accepted as a shorthand way of pointing to their preoccupation with mortal sin, damnation, and Hell. But if Greene learnt something from Mauriac at this stage of his career it was not an influence that persisted after he drew away from Catholic themes. Hence, perhaps, his discouraging response to later interviewers on the subject. Being unwilling to regard himself as a 'Catholic novelist', he needed to distance himself from a writer who was widely acclaimed as precisely that.

In Greene's *Collected Essays* there are short studies of Léon Bloy, who provided an epigraph for *The End of the Affair*, and of Georges Bernanos, as well as the one on Mauriac. He kept up an intelligent interest in French Catholic writing, as he did in many other subjects, and the French have long been enthusiastic readers of his work, producing critical studies of him before anglophone readers did. In 1953 Greene's *Essais Catholiques* appeared in France, a translated collection which, as well as more recent pieces, included 'Henry James: the Religious Aspect', showing that he still upheld the ideas in that early essay. Meanwhile, Greene was passing through a religious crisis and Evelyn Waugh reported him as saying in that year that he 'was no longer a practising Catholic'.[15] He later wrote 'in the years between *The Heart of the Matter* and *The End of the Affair* I felt myself used and exhausted by the victims of religion'. In fact, Greene continued to regard himself as some kind of a Catholic for the rest of his life, as his biographers have described. It is not a topic I shall pursue further, since my primary interest is in the work and not the life.

An eminent Catholic novelist, Muriel Spark, has declared that there is no such thing as a 'Catholic novel', and George Orwell thought that Catholics were unlikely to be any good at writing novels: 'The atmosphere of orthodoxy is always damaging to prose, and above all it is completely ruinous to the novel, the most anarchical of all forms of literature. How many Roman Catholics have been good novelists? Even the handful one could name have usually been bad Catholics. The novel is practically a Protestant form of art; it is a product of the free mind, of the autonomous individual.'[16] Orwell takes a narrowly Protestant and English view of the matter. There have been quite a number of English Catholic novelists, some of them good, as Thomas Woodman shows in his informative study, *Faithful Fictions: The Catholic Novel in British Literature* (1991). The example of Mauriac shows how the tension between orthodoxy and individual desire can prove creative. And one of the greatest of European novels, Alessandro Manzoni's *The Betrothed* (*I Promessi Sposi*), of which the final version appeared in 1840, is entirely permeated by Catholicism. It is set in the turbulent society of northern Italy in the early seventeenth century, and though Manzoni's starting point is the historical fiction of Scott, his capacity for fierce, uncompromising realism, as in the descriptions of famine and plague in Milan, looks forward to Zola. Manzoni combined Catholic devotion with Enlightenment tolerance and scepticism. He was writing in and for a totally Catholic culture, and this sharply distinguishes him from English Catholic novelists, who were part of an embattled minority in a society that was strongly Protestant and anti-papist (and became increasingly secular in later years); and from those in France, where the national religion was notionally Catholic, but where intellectual life was dominated by the anticlericalism of the Revolutionary and Republican tradition.

There is sufficient evidence to undermine Orwell's claim. Nevertheless, there are philosophical rather than historical grounds for questioning the extent to which any religious belief, and not just Catholicism, can really be at home in the novel. As a literary form it has usually been thought of as this-worldly, realistic, empirical, dealing with people rather like ourselves, 'low mimetic' in Northrop Frye's term. Unlike the romance, it was not well adapted to supernatural interventions; if religion appeared it was likely to be as a matter of social behaviour, as with the clergymen of Trollope or J. F. Powers, or a source of individual ethical conviction. And this is broadly true of Manzoni's novel, though all the characters, whether heroes, saints, or villains, are Catholics. Writers like Bernanos and Mauriac, and Greene in his last Catholic novel, who are concerned with grace and divine intervention in the life of the individual soul, are to some extent working against the grain of the form, though the attempt can be profitable. This was true above all of Dostoevsky, a defiant Christian in what he condemned as an age of unbelief, who used the realistic novel as an arena for the struggle between belief and unbelief, salvation and damnation. Orwell believed that the 'atmosphere of orthodoxy' was damaging to prose; Dostoevsky showed that the atmosphere of Orthodoxy could produce great novels. He did not like Catholicism, but it is not surprising that Bernanos and Mauriac acknowledged their debt to him. Greene did not; indeed, the only reference to Dostoevsky that I can recall in his essays is circumspect and ambiguous. At the end of 'Henry James: The Religious Aspect', he remarks of James's novels, 'They retain their beautiful symmetry at a price, the price which Turgenev paid and Dostoevsky refused to pay, the price of adding to the novelist's distinction that of a philosopher or a religious teacher of the second rank.' It is not altogether clear whether Greene thinks it is right for the novelist to pay this price. Certainly he was not indebted to Dostoevsky in the way that the French novelists were; but there are recurring places in his work where I am reminded of Dostoevsky, for positive or negative reasons. When at the end of *It's a Battlefield* the prison chaplain says one can't hand in one's resignation to God he—or the author—seems to be alluding to Ivan Karamazov's attempt to do just that. In the opening of *A Gun for Sale* Raven climbs a staircase and commits two murders, just as Raskolnikov does in *Crime and Punishment*. The interrogation of the priest by the police lieutenant in *The Power and the Glory* has affinities with the encounter of the Grand Inquisitor and Christ in *The Brothers Karamazov*. Bendrix's outbursts of articulate hatred echo those of the Underground Man. As I have suggested, it would have taken Dostoevsky to present Rose Wilson or Henry Scobie in their human depth. There is, too, the remark in Greene's appreciative essay on Bernanos that he wishes he could have been one of the original readers of *Sous le Soleil de Satan* when it appeared in 1926: 'With what astonishment, in this novel unlike all novels hitherto, they must have encountered *le tueur d'âmes* when he intercepted the curé on the dark road to Boulaincourt in the guise of a little lubricious horse-dealer with his sinister gaiety and his horrible affection and his grotesque playfulness.' Had Greene forgotten that well before Bernanos wrote, the Devil had had a lengthy discussion with Ivan Karamazov? A twentieth-century novelist who needs to be mentioned in this context is the Japanese Catholic Shusaku Endo, whose *Silence* (1969) was described by Greene as 'one of the finest novels of our time'. The setting is Japan in the early seventeenth century, where Catholicism, introduced by Jesuit missionaries, has taken root and flourished. But government policy changes and a savage persecution ensues. The missionary priests are given the option of apostatizing and being spared to live a quiet life in Japan, or having their flocks tortured to death. They have to reject God in order to spare others, and to endure the rest of their lives in his silence. It is a passive form of Job's dilemma; and it goes more deeply than Greene into questions raised in *The Power and the Glory. Silence* is an extraordinarily powerful novel which deserves Greene's high praise. And though not conventionally edifying its spirit is deeply Catholic.

The novels that Greene wrote between 1938 and 1951 placed him into the category of 'Catholic novelist', however much he resisted it, in the company of his friend Waugh and their French co-religionists, Bernanos and Mauriac. Waugh encouraged such a presentation of Greene, in ways he later came to regret. When he was lecturing in North American universities in 1949, he delivered an account of Chesterton, Greene, and Ronald Knox as three English writers with very different backgrounds and temperaments who were agreed on the essentials of belief. All three were converts, like Waugh, and by the fact of lecturing on them he appeared as part of the team. His biographer, Martin Stannard, describes the lecture as 'a show-stopper. Packed houses greeted him everywhere—and he did not disappoint them.' Waugh had the temperament of a showman, unlike the reclusive and evasive Greene. Despite his reservations about the theology of *The Heart of the Matter*, Waugh inserted a couple of product-placing references to it in *Men at Arms*, the first volume of his military trilogy; he took one of them out in 1965 when he revised the trilogy into a one-volume work under the title of *Sword of Honour*. After the publication of *The End of the Affair* Greene was determined to escape from the category of 'Catholic novelist'. He told Waugh that he was thinking of writing a political novel (which was to be *The Quiet American*): 'It will be fun to write about politics for a change, and not always about God.' To which Waugh memorably replied, 'I wouldn't give up writing about God at this stage if I was you. It would be like P. G. Wodehouse dropping Jeeves half-way through the Wooster series.'[17]

NOTES

1. M.-F. Allain, *The Other Man* (Harmondsworth, 1984), 161–2.
2. Martin Stannard, *Evelyn Waugh: No Abiding City 1939–66* (London, 1992), 216n.
3. E. Waugh, *Essays* (London, 1983), 360–6.
4. In S. Hynes (ed.), *Graham Greene* (Englewood Cliffs, NJ, 1973), 103–4.
5. *Times Literary Supplement*, 3 September 2004.
6. Donat O'Donnell [pseudonym of Conor Cruise O'Brien], *Maria Cross: Imaginative Patterns in a Group of Modern Catholic Writers* (London, 1953), 66.
7. Ian Gregor, 'The End of the Affair' in Hynes, *Greene*, 110–26.
8. R. Sharrock, *Saints, Sinners and Comedians* (Tunbridge Wells, 1984), 161.
9. D. Lodge, *The Novelist at the Crossroads* (London, 1971), 32.
10. In Hynes, *Greene*, 127.
11. Waugh, *Essays*, 404–6.
12. In Hynes, *Greene* 136.
13. Ibid. 161.
14. K. Allott and M. Ferris, *The Art of Graham Greene* (London, 1951), 25n.
15. Evelyn Waugh, *Diaries*, ed. Michael Davie (Harmondsworth, 1979), 721.
16. In Orwell's essay 'Inside the Whale', available in several collections of his work.
17. Christopher Sykes, *Evelyn Waugh* (London, 1975), 357.

7
The Greene Man

GREENE liked putting the word 'man' in his titles: *The Man Within,
The Third Man, Our Man in Havana, The Tenth Man, No Man's Land.*
In this spirit Marie-Françoise Allain called her collection of inter-
views with him *The Other Man* and the first chapter 'The Secret
Man'. I continue the tradition in the title of this chapter, which
gestures towards Greene's interest in things that are green, and in
persons named Green or Greene. Specifically, it recalls the Green
Man, the pub in *It's a Battlefield* where Conder meets the policeman
Patmore. Maurice Bendrix is the first of the clearly identifiable
Greene Men, though there are hints of them in D. and Arthur Rowe
and Henry Scobie. Indeed, Norman Sherry, who loses no opportunity to identify Greene and his characters, remarks exaggeratedly
that Scobie 'is almost a clone of Greene himself'. Like many of
Greene's characters, Scobie is deeply weary and longs for peace; but
he lacks the world-weariness, the cynicism, the experience with
women, and the sexual jealousy that belongs to the fully-formed
Greene Man. I am indebted to Sherry for pointing me towards this
concept, even though I deplore his readiness to reduce novels to the
raw material of biography. He is specific and comprehensive in his
identifications: 'Morin is Greene. Querry is Greene'. 'Greene is
Bendrix; Greene is Brown . . .'. 'Plarr . . . is yet another of Greene's
burnt-out cases'.[1] Greene would not have liked any of this; he hotly
contested Evelyn Waugh's assumption that Querry's spiritual

plight in *A Burnt Out Case* reflected Greene's own, insisting, in traditional terms, that an author should not be identified with his character. In principle, he was right, though a novelist's account of what he is doing in a text has no necessarily privileged status. Sherry is writing as a biographer rather than a literary critic, but even by current norms of biographical writing there is something tactless and indecorous in his approach. He writes, 'Though most of his leading characters are offshoots of Greene, no character is released and separate—they are chained to him.'[2] On the face of it this is a severe judgement, indicating a sharp decline in inventiveness, though it is not one that Sherry attempts to enforce in his reading of Greene's later career. I have to say, at the risk of being involved in contradiction, first, that there is a disturbing truth in this analysis, and secondly, that it is not the whole truth, and that Greene may need to be rescued from his devoted biographer.

The End of the Affair was a significantly transitional work. It was Greene's last appearance as a committed Catholic novelist, and his last novel for many years to have an English setting. The first-person narrative was an innovation in his work, and he told Allain that this novel and *The Quiet American* represented a transition to a simpler style. He also said that *The End of the Affair* and *Travels with my Aunt* were his only novels that avoided melodrama, by which he meant a measure of violence in the action.* One could put this point differently by remarking that *The End of the Affair*, the austere and adult tale of passion, is unique in Greene's novels in showing no trace of the adventure stories and thrillers that influenced his fiction, early and late. And with Bendrix the Greene Man takes centre stage for the first time. (I am not assuming that these characters are all versions of their author, simply that they have family resemblances with each other, and with the persona of Greene that emerges from

---

* Not true, anyway. Wordsworth dies violently at the end of the latter novel.

his writings.) *The Quiet American* was the political novel that Greene embarked on as a change from writing about God. After the restricted London setting of *The End of the Affair* it is a move to the foreign parts that many readers now regard as the essential territory of Greeneland. After the war he travelled widely, both personally and in the scenes of his fiction. *The Quiet American* reflects several visits in the early 1950s to Indochina, where the French were fighting a doomed war in defence of their Far Eastern colony against nationalists and communists, of whom the most celebrated was Ho Chi Minh. Zadie Smith finds this novel contains 'great journalism'; at that time Greene was active as a journalist, writing extensively about the French Indochina war for English, French, and American publications, whilst gathering material for his novel, which has obvious journalistic virtues. As narrated by the veteran newspaperman Thomas Fowler, the account is plain, direct, and forceful, particularly in the descriptions of battle and atrocity. At first glance *The Quiet American* presents an evident contrast to *The End of the Affair*; Saigon under terrorist attack is more vividly evoked than London under the flying bombs, and whilst Greene confesses that he had trouble in sustaining Bendrix's first-person narrative, Fowler's seems effortless. Fowler is the second of the Greene Men, less consumed with hatred than Bendrix and with more decent impulses, but subject to the same weariness and cynicism. Despite the differences in scene and atmosphere, and leaving aside the political dimension, structural resemblances between the two novels are noticeable. Both involve a love triangle; if Bendrix loses Sarah to God, Fowler loses his Vietnamese mistress Phuong to the Quiet American, Alden Pyle. Though *The Quiet American* does not attempt the Fordian complexities of time-scheme in *The End of the Affair*, it presents a calculated chronology, beginning with the murder of Pyle, and using the rest of the novel to show who he was, what he did, and what happened to him.

The Quiet American has long been admired as a political novel, exposing the destructive effects of the well-meaning American innocence embodied in Pyle, and anticipating the long and disastrous involvement in Vietnam when the Americans took over the anti-communist fight from the French, and subsequent US wars and military adventures. That significance is certainly there, and it has developed since the novel was published, in the familiar process whereby literary works acquire fresh meanings as they move into new historical situations and encounter the expectations of new readers. But Greene did not write it as a Cold War novel; indeed, here as elsewhere, it is hard to identify the author's political stance. It is not an obviously anti-colonialist work; the desperate French struggle to retain this portion of their empire is shown as failing, but it is regarded with some sympathy. The dedicated though disillusioned French officers, commanding native troops and mostly German Foreign Legionaries, are more impressive than the Americans, who as yet are involved in the war only marginally and covertly, and who are condemned by the French for not sending promised military supplies. Vigot, the French police officer in Saigon, is admired for his skill and professionalism, like previous policemen in Greene's novels; he is a cultivated man who reads Pascal in his office. (Greene may be making a friendly gesture to the Pascalian Mauriac.) So, too, is Fowler, who quotes Baudelaire and Clough. Fowler, like Greene, is forcefully anti-American, but the hostility was cultural rather than political. Greene had expressed his dislike in film reviews of the 1930s, which derided the crassness and vulgarity of Hollywood productions and praised the artistically serious works of the French and Russian cinema. In *The Lawless Roads* Greene describes coming across some American women's magazines and being disgusted by their vacuity and banality, which pointed to something worse than all that he disliked in Mexico: 'Here were idolatry and oppression, starvation and casual violence, but you lived under the shadow of religion—of God or the Devil. "Rating for Dating"—it wasn't evil, it wasn't anything at all, it was just the drugstore and the Coca-Cola, the hamburger, the sinless graceless chromium world.' Greene's hostility was that of a traditional European conservative, in contrast to the later attitudes of the global Left, which excoriated American political behaviour whilst accepting American popular culture: Coca-Cola, hamburgers, baseball caps, movies, jazz, and rock.

After Pyle's death Fowler is asked to identify his body in a police mortuary, where he seems more out of place than ever. He thinks that Pyle should have stayed at home, and identifies him with the culture that produced him: 'I saw him in a family snapshot album, riding on a dude ranch, bathing on Long Island, photographed with his colleagues in some apartment on the twenty-third floor. He belonged to the skyscraper and the express lift, the ice-cream and the dry Martinis, milk at lunch, and chicken sandwiches on the Merchant Limited.' Later, at a moment of great distress—Phuong has abandoned him for Pyle—Fowler goes into the Men's Room at the US legation and starts to cry, but his tears are thwarted by one of the great innovations of American civilization: 'Even their lavatories were air-conditioned, and presently the temperate tempered air dried my tears as it dries the spit in your mouth and the seed in your body.'

Pyle is presented as a product of his culture, rather than as a character of any complexity or depth. And that, Greene seems to be implying, is the whole point about him. He is brash, ill-informed, self-confident, and courageous to the point of foolhardiness. Fowler has many reasons to dislike him even before he steals Phuong. But then Pyle saves his life. They are travelling in the battle zone in the north of the country when their car breaks down at night in an area dominated after dark by communist guerrillas. They are attacked and Fowler is wounded; Pyle carries him through a swamp and eventually they are rescued. The episode is described in a taut, compelling prose which recalls Greene's early debt to adventure stories. Fowler responds with gratitude and makes determined attempts to reciprocate Pyle's high regard for him. He accepts the loss of Phuong, recognizing that Pyle is a younger man with much more to offer her, particularly marriage and a life in America. Fowler cannot offer to marry Phuong, as his wife in England, from whom he has been long separated, is a strict Anglo-Catholic and does not believe in divorce.

Phuong is a beautiful girl but a shadowy fictional character, whose exoticism both defines and conceals her. The relationship between her and Fowler is plausibly presented by Greene, but is clearly a precarious union of totally different worlds. Significantly, she and Fowler communicate in French, the language of the imperial power (and one which Pyle barely speaks). One of Phuong's services to Fowler is preparing him pipes of opium; he finds the drug a comfort, though he is not addicted. Among other things it sustains his detachment from the world around him. As a reporter his role is to investigate and describe what is happening, not to make judgements about events and still less to change anything. As Fowler discovers more about Pyle's activities, he has to reassess this stance. Pyle, inspired by an academic guru in the United States, is convinced that the future of Vietnam lies with a Third Force, which will be neither communist nor imperialist. With his characteristic energy and narrow vision, he is trying to set one up, having identified a suitable leader in a local warlord with a private army. Pyle arranges to supply them with weapons and explosives. But things go horribly wrong when this favoured group explodes a bomb in a crowded street and kills fifty people. Greene lets Fowler describe this atrocity in a flat, painfully observant style that has the quality of the best journalism. This event shakes Fowler out of his habitual detachment; he decides that Pyle will have to go before he does any more damage. He uses his contacts to meet a member of the communist underground and warn him about Pyle. Fowler does not want him to be killed, indeed hopes that he can somehow be removed from the scene without violence, but Pyle is murdered. We read in the first chapter how his body is recovered from the river after he has been stabbed to death. The episode, and Fowler's ambiguous responsibility for the death, are reminiscent of the sequence in *The Heart of the Matter* in which Scobie's servant Ali is murdered.

The Quiet American, the novel in which Greene decided to give God a rest, has a humanistic rather than a religious frame of reference. It raises the questions about human motives and responsibilities which are the common material of serious post-Christian novels (the kind that Greene had attacked in his essay on Mauriac for their insufficient sense of human nature). But God is not easily excluded from the world, and he makes an unexpected appearance in the novel. Towards the end of the story the journalist Granger, a noisy American whom Fowler detests, confides to him in some distress at a party that he has just heard that his young son, back in the United States, is suffering from polio. 'Do you know what I've been doing in there while that bastard was singing? I was praying. I thought maybe if God wanted a life he could take mine.' Granger does not know if he believes in God, but that at this point he wishes he did. The motif of offering one's life for someone else ('substitution' in theological terms) occurs elsewhere in Greene's writing, as in *The Power and the Glory* and *The Potting Shed*.

The novel moves to a grimly happy ending. After Pyle's death Phuong returns to Fowler, and renews her wish to marry him. Fowler's wife Helen sends him a telegram saying she has thought better of her refusal to divorce to him and is making the necessary arrangements. So he will marry Phuong and take her to England, a country she knows only from reading magazine articles about the Royal Family. But she is ready to accept Cheddar Gorge rather than the Grand Canyon. Fowler's final memory of Pyle associates him with an artefact of American mass culture: 'I thought of the first day and Pyle sitting beside me at the Continental, with his eye on the soda-fountain across the way. Everything had gone right with me since he died, but how I wished there existed someone to whom I could say that I was sorry.' God is the someone the unbelieving Fowler wishes for, *Deus absconditus* casting a shadow at the end. *The Quiet American* deserves its reputation both as a political novel and as a love story. It is in its way a faultless work, finely controlled and consistent in tone. If I have reservations about it, it is because I miss the characteristics of the faulty earlier works: the poetry, the contrast and combination of literary strands, the wayward energy, the outbreaks of melodrama, the intrusive grotesques who rock the boat of the narrative. Nevertheless, it showed the path on which Greene was now set as a novelist and which he would follow for the rest of his career. His next novel, *Our Man in Havana*, was one of his rare ventures into comic fiction and was well received. I shall defer discussion of it until later, in order to continue pursuing the Greene Man.

He appears as a renegade Catholic in a short story, 'A Visit to Morin', first published in a magazine in 1957, and in *A Burnt Out Case*. The story is narrated by Dunlop, an Englishman in the wine trade who is a dedicated reader of French literature, and has long admired the novels of a famous Catholic writer, Pierre Morin. Travelling in France one Christmas, he attends Midnight Mass in a village church, though he is not himself a Catholic. He knows that Morin lives in the area and he recognizes him in the congregation. After Mass he introduces himself and the elderly writer invites him back to his house to sample some wine of which he is proud. Dunlop tells Morin that he has long admired his novels, and is both shocked and fascinated when Morin says that his Catholicism has now virtually disappeared; Dunlop had indeed been surprised at Mass that Morin had not received Communion like the rest of the

congregation. The two men engage in one of the prolonged noc-
turnal discussions that are a recurring motif in Greene's fiction.
Morin reveals himself as weary, bored, cynical, a characteristic
Greene Man. He has been particularly turned off by his fame as a
Catholic, when he received many letters from devout admirers:
' "Long after I had ceased to believe myself I was a carrier of belief,
like a man can be a carrier of disease without being sick. Women
especially." He added with disgust, "I had only to sleep with a
woman to make a convert."' Morin's rejection of the burden of
being a famous Catholic writer is close to Greene's own, when he
wrote in *Ways of Escape* 'I felt myself used and exhausted by the victims of religion.' Morin is in the paradoxical situation of having lost
belief whilst still having faith in the truth of the Church. But he is
afraid to resume Catholic practice in case his belief does not return.
In his discussions with Marie-Françoise Allain, Greene proposed a
similar paradox, rejecting 'belief' in particular Catholic doctrines
and devotional practices whilst maintaining 'faith' in the basic truth
of the whole. It is traditional Catholic teaching that whoever gives
up the practice of the faith will suffer in some way; for Greene, and
Morin, the suffering somehow implies the truth of the faith.

Morin's situation has affinities with Greene's own at that time,
though he resisted any idea of a total identification with his character. In fact he seems to have drawn on François Mauriac for aspects
of Morin. Mauriac was a Catholic novelist of whom it could be said,
as it was of Morin, 'He had offended the orthodox Catholics in his
own country and pleased the liberal Catholics abroad'. Like both
Greene and Mauriac, Morin has been accused of being (or at least
described as) a Jansenist and an Augustinian. The titles of Morin's
novels have a Mauriacan ring: *Le Diable au Ciel* and *Le Bien Pensant*.
Whether there was, in Greene's intentions, any more of Mauriac in
Morin than these external aspects is unknown and in any case not
relevant. What one can say is that Greene inserted into the narrative

of 'A Visit to Morin' a few easily deciphered personal signals. Dunlop remembers Mr Strangeways, the Catholic schoolmaster who had introduced him to Morin's novels, resisting speculation about the novelist's personal belief with the words, 'A novel is made up of words and characters. Are the words well chosen and do the characters live? All the rest belongs to literary gossip. You are not in this class to learn how to be gossip-writers.' The mass of biography directed at Greene was still in the future, but he could probably sense its approach. We are told that, among Morin's hostile readers, 'The word "paradox" was frequently used with an air of disapproval.' Greene would have recalled that when the Vatican authorities tried to condemn *The Power and the Glory* recourse to paradox was one of the charges against it.

'A Visit to Morin' is a highly accomplished story, where serious themes are presented briefly, with a light touch. But when Greene returned to them at greater length in *A Burnt Out Case* he produced what is, I believe, one of his weakest novels. It is a return to Africa, to what was still—just—known as the Belgian Congo. In *The Lawless Roads* he had written that Mexico 'was something that I couldn't shake off, like a state of mind.' In the dedicatory letter of *A Burnt Out Case* he remarks, 'This Congo is a region of the mind.' Any writer's chosen territory must, in a sense, be a state of mind, to be reconstructed in words from memory and feeling and imagination. But Greene's Mexico is far more substantially realized than his Congo. The central figure of *A Burnt Out Case*, Querry, is a further embodiment of the Greene Man. Like Morin, he is a famous Catholic artist who is bored and disgusted with his reputation and who has largely given up believing in Catholicism. He is, though, not a novelist but an architect who has achieved fame with his ecclesiastical buildings. This strikes me as an initial false touch. Architects can indeed achieve celebrity, and the idea of a famous Catholic architect is not absurd. But novelists can acquire a reputation where their readers feel their problems are being personally addressed by the author and wish to discuss them further with him. This is what Morin had found, and so did Greene. Greene vehemently denied that he in any sense 'was Querry', being prepared to admit no more than that his character may have shared some of his attributes. In fact Querry has a similar temperament to Greene, and his career has passed through similar stages of fame, such as being portrayed on the cover of *Time* magazine. The lack of detachment is unmistakable, more so than with any other of the Greene Men.

Greene's friend Evelyn Waugh disliked *A Burnt Out Case* and declined to review it. He made a harsh but precise summary in his diary: 'The hero of *A Burnt Out Case* is a bored, loveless voluptuary who hides his despair in the most remote place he can find—a leper settlement in the Congo—recovers a spark of humanity but not his "faith" and dies in an absurdly melodramatic way.'[3] Waugh was distressed by the book because he felt that, combined with 'A Visit to Morin', it showed that Greene was abandoning Catholicism, though in their ensuing correspondence Greene strongly denied this. Writing as a practitioner Waugh probes the many weak points in the novel: 'Graham's skill is fading. He describes the hero's predicament three times, once, painfully, in a "fairy story" which is supposed to take up a whole night but is in fact told in ten minutes. The incident of Deo Gratias' attempted escape and rescue is poorly handled.'

The best parts of the novel are in the opening account of Querry's voyage up river through the jungle to the leper settlement. It is a forceful description which recalls without being actually derived from *Heart of Darkness*, which Greene had been rereading. But Greene's Congo has none of the hallucinatory power of his Mexico. The community of priests who run the leper settlement where Querry retreats is sympathetically described, and the unbelieving doctor in charge of the hospital is presented as admirable. Early in the story Querry recalls saying in a dream, 'I am sorry, I am too far gone, I can't feel at all, I am a leper.' He seeks the isolation from the world that was the traditional lot of lepers. They have already made figurative appearances in Greene's fiction. In *The Heart of the Matter* it is said of the garrulous, loud-voiced Father Rank, 'he swung his great empty-sounding bell to and fro, Ho, ho, ho, like a leper proclaiming his misery'; in *The Quiet American* Fowler observes, 'innocence is like a dumb leper who has lost his bell, wandering the world meaning no harm'. The latter-day lepers whom Querry encounters are not in such a desperate plight, as modern medicine can, in principle, cure the disease. Those sufferers in whom it has been arrested after they have suffered distressing mutilations are known as 'burnt-out cases'. This is how Querry sees himself. Greene had to face—and failed—the challenge of making a hollow man the central figure in a novel without seeming hollow and unconvincing as a character. Querry lacks the dynamic hatred of Bendrix, or the weary but strong attachment to his career of Fowler; unlike them he does not establish his presence in a first-person narrative. There is, in James's terms, much more telling than showing in *A Burnt Out Case*. In earlier novels Greene had made effective use of free indirect style, where a character's thoughts are revealed in a third-person narrative, with occasional interventions and expansions by the author. But Greene refuses to use this device in this novel; indeed, in 'Congo Journal', included in *In Search of a Character*, he perversely insists that the author 'should not penetrate into the thoughts of any character—which must be indicated only in action and dialogue'. The journal shows the difficulties Greene experienced in planning the novel; at the beginning he knew no more than that it would be about an unknown man who somehow turns up in the heart of the Congo. Many good novels have emerged from such tenuous beginnings, but Greene's uncertainty of aim affected the finished work. It may be significant that for a long time he could not think of a name for his central character, referring to him only as 'X'. At a later stage he decided on 'Querry', a portmanteau name which combines 'quarry' and 'query'. Not wanting to make him a writer, Greene eventually decided that he could be an architect. But when Querry is describing his profession to Dr Colin he presents it in literary terms: 'Materials are the architect's plot. They are not his motive for work. Only the space and the light and the proportion. The subject of a novel is not the plot.'

Apart from Querry, there are missed opportunities in *A Burnt Out Case*. Greene has always been skilled at inventing fascinatingly nasty characters, and there are several here, particularly Rycker, a Belgian *colon* who manages a margarine factory. He is a former seminarian, assertive and pharisaically Catholic, who pursues and flatters Querry because of his fame. Rycker has lovelessly married a young girl, Marie, in the spirit of the Pauline injunction that it is better to marry than to burn. She, at the end, falls in love with Querry, with fatal results. There is Father Thomas, the one unattractive member of the priestly community, who is both insecure and authoritarian by temperament. And there is the travelling English journalist Montague Parkinson, obese and odious, with his total indifference to the truth of the stories he writes, and his stock of misattributed literary quotations. The earlier Greene would have done much more with these figures, turning them into gross but entertaining caricatures who dominated the scenes in which they appeared. In this novel they merely come and go. There is a real potential for comedy in the scenes in which Querry tries to convince first Rycker and then Thomas that he is no longer a believing Catholic, that he wants to get away from the Church and his reputation, that nothing means very much to him any more. But they will not believe him, treating these explanations as examples of 'aridity', the theological name for the desolate condition in which the soul wrongly believes it has been deserted by God, or simply as signs of a profound humility. Commenting on the novel in *Ways of Escape*, Greene remarked that both Marxist and Catholic readers 'were too concerned with faith or no faith to notice that in the course of the blackest book I have written I had discovered Comedy'. Greene may have discovered it, but he did not get it into the book. On the evidence this novel presents one might have concluded that he himself was something of a burnt-out case; but he had another thirty years of life and work ahead of him.

The Greene Man next appears as Brown, the narrator of *The Comedians* (like Querry, he is mononominal). In the opening of the novel we meet him on board ship with companions named Jones and Smith; these are the three commonest surnames in English, and Greene the joker obviously enjoyed setting up this group; as I have remarked, the name Brown had some special significance for him, with or without a final 'e'. The three travellers are bound for Haiti, the black republic in the Caribbean that has always been notorious for extreme poverty and civic corruption and which at this time, the early sixties, has been brought even lower by the savage dictatorship of Papa Doc Duvalier. Brown tells the story, in a return by Greene to first-person narrative. He owns a hotel on the island which he had inherited from his mother and which for a time had done well out of the tourist trade. But now it shares the prevalent running down of life, for Duvalier has scared away the tourists; in an unsuccessful attempt to sell the hotel, Brown has been to New York, from where he is now returning. Jones is an English con man and soldier of fortune who has been on a dubious mission in the Congo and hopes to find ways of enriching himself in the disrupted society of Haiti. Smith is an elderly American, a tireless supporter of liberal causes, who has the distinction of having once stood on the ticket of the Vegetarian Party in a presidential election in the United States. He is travelling to Haiti with his formidable wife on a mad quixotic mission, to set up a centre to further the vegetarian cause.

The Comedians continues the interest in Latin America that Greene had started in Mexico and continued in Cuba and was to pursue in several more books. This novel also shares a characteristic with *The Quiet American* and *A Burnt Out Case*, in that Haiti, like colonial Vietnam and the Belgian Congo, is French-speaking, and the central figure in each is an Englishman who converses in French for much of the story. In *The Comedians* there are references to Baudelaire and Edith Piaf and French pop singers of the sixties. This motif is a curiosity rather than anything of serious thematic interest, and reflects the way in which Greene felt at home in French culture; he went to live permanently in France at about the time the novel appeared.

Brown has failed in his mission but he is not altogether sorry to be returning to Haiti, despite the danger and desolation of the country. He preserves a certain attachment to the place; more urgently, he wants to see his mistress, Martha, the German wife of a Latin American diplomat in the capital, Port au Prince. Her father had been a Nazi, hanged after the war for war crimes, while Brown's French mother had served in the Resistance. The authorial joker is at work in these symmetries. Brown is a pure example of the Greene Man, weary, cynical, rootless and tormented by sexual jealousy. He is outside his hotel as the sun rises: 'The first colours touched the garden, deep green and then deep red—transience was my pigmentation; my roots would never go deep enough anywhere to make me a home or make me secure with love.' But Brown, unlike his predecessors, has a sense of humour, even though he says of himself that he has 'never learnt the trick of laughter'. His story brings out the ways in which horror turns into farce; usually black farce, if that is not an incorrect description in such a context. There are some authentically comic episodes, reflecting the side of Greene that had produced *Our Man in Havana*. The horror, though, is dominant; the reader is made cruelly aware of the disease and poverty of the Haitian people; as in the account of the hordes of beggars, many of them hideously mutilated, who besiege customers at the principal post office. There is general fear of the sinister Tontons Macoutes, Duvalier's secret police, who always wear dark glasses and drive through the streets arresting people at random. The mortality rate is very high, even for a Greene novel. At the end of the book most of the Haitian characters are dead, including one of the most horrible, Captain Concasseur, and one of the most likeable, Dr Magiot, a physician who strives to act decently amid the dominant cruelty and corruption. He is inspired by a vaguely idealistic Marxism which is concerned not with the present realities of Communism but with an ultimate better future for humanity. There are other likeable characters, particularly Mr Smith. He embodies the qualities that Greene dislikes in Americans and had embodied in Alden Pyle: the blundering innocence that does more harm than good, the profound ignorance of other forms of life and culture. And yet he is clearly a good man, for all his absurdity, with the courage to be outraged by the prevailing horrors and to try to do something about them. The attractive presentation of Smith and his wife suggests a certain mellowing of Greene's prejudices. The third member of the party, Jones, is a self-serving villain whose claims about himself are steadily deflated, but he is an amiably comic figure, with the power to make people laugh. He mildly recalls Greene's early taste for the buffoons and humours of Elizabethan comedy.

The Comedians has been described as a political novel, but as with earlier novels by Greene that have attracted this label it is not easy to know what the political dimensions are. There is an emerging resistance movement against Duvalier's tyranny which produces some gunplay towards the end of the novel, and there is talk of an invasion from the neighbouring Dominican Republic. But there is none of the serious concern with political issues that occurs in

Dostoevsky and Conrad (and to take a later instance, Arthur Koestler's *Darkness at Noon*). *The Comedians* is an adventure story, a return to the genre that inspired Greene in his boyhood, full of violence and fear and rapid movement and lashings of local colour; these qualities are given an adult topping in Brown's joyless affair with Martha, who is no more convincing than most of Greene's female characters (though her demonic small son Angel is a terrifying presence, who might have dominated the story if we had seen more of him). It is a technically competent novel, showing none of the weaknesses and uncertainties of *A Burnt Out Case*, perhaps because Greene was no longer dealing with problematical religious issues. There may be a suggestion of them in Brown's recollections of his education by the Jesuits, but he is firm in his unbelief. In an essay published in the 1980s I described *The Comedians* as 'undoubtedly one of his finest novels'. I think that was excessive; I would now describe it as an accomplished adventure story, which touches on serious matters in its rapid movement but does not get caught up in any of them.

In *The Honorary Consul* Greene returned to the Hispanic regions of Latin America, though there is an echo of the Haitian experience in a reference to the fall from power of Papa Doc. This novel shows the Greene Men beginning to resemble each other ever more closely. The central character, Doctor Eduardo Plarr, is cynical and infinitely weary of himself and the world, and one is surprised to know that he is only in his early thirties. He is given to sour and knowing reflections about life in the manner of French moralists: 'One cannot love oneself, one cannot live for long close to oneself—everyone has need of a stranger in the bed, and a whore remains a stranger. Her body has been scrawled over by so many men you can never decipher your own signature there.' He has many affinities with Brown in *The Comedians*. He is an ex-Catholic, now an unbeliever, who was educated in a Jesuit school. His father was

English, his mother foreign (French in Brown's case, Paraguayan in Plarr's). He retains British citizenship, but has long lived as an expatriate in Argentina. Like Brown, he is having an affair with the wife of a diplomat (though that is to stretch the term; the cuckold is only a British honorary consul, though he likes to give himself the airs of someone grander). Plarr is a doctor who has moved from Buenos Aires to practise in a northern provincial city on the border with Paraguay, where his long absent father is believed to be a political prisoner of the dictator General Stroessner. Plarr embodies another recurring type in Greene's later novels, the dedicated physician who does what he can to cure the poor and oppressed, like Dr Colin in *A Burnt Out Case* and Dr Magiot in *The Comedians*. But, despite the good he does in the world, he avoids expressing any idealistic feelings about it.

The starting point of the narrative would make a grimly comic short story. A group of leftist guerrillas plans to kidnap the American ambassador when he is on an official visit to the area; their intention is to put pressure on General Stroessner to release a number of prisoners, including Plarr senior. The leader of the guerrillas is León Rivas, who was a schoolfriend of Eduardo Plarr. He had trained as a lawyer and then become a priest. Under the influence of Liberation Theology he has abandoned the priesthood, whilst continuing to believe in a certain amount of Catholic doctrine, and has plunged into the armed struggle against capitalism and imperialism. Rivas is eloquent and talks a lot but he is one of those characters Greene complained about who never properly come alive. Rivas and his group are sadly incompetent, for they bungle the kidnapping; instead of the American ambassador they abduct the local British honorary consul, an insignificant figure who has no leverage value on the international scene. Furthermore, he is not well regarded by his employers, and the British Foreign Office is moving towards ending his appointment.

The Consul, Charley Fortnum, is an expatriate businessman now in his sixties, who has taken on the consulship, partly for prestige and partly because of the financial perks it brings him. He is an amiable character, and convincingly drawn in a broad-brush, caricatural way. He is addicted to the whisky bottle, and as a widower he has married a young prostitute, Clara, who is several decades younger than himself; this marriage makes him a figure of fun in the locality, and adds to his bad record at the Embassy in Buenos Aires. Clara combines two of Greene's recurring types, the waif and the whore, though as the very young wife of a much older man she has affinities with Marie Rycker in *A Burnt Out Case*. Plarr embarks on an affair with her and she becomes pregnant with his child, though for most of the narrative Charley believes it is his. At the end of the novel he is alive and Plarr and Rivas are not.

Echoes of Greene's previous novels are frequently apparent, and not only in characterization. Like much of his later fiction, it gives an impression of being skilfully put together from prefabricated elements. Greene's obsessive joking is evident in two minor characters called Henry, Eduardo Parr's absent father, and the British ambassador to Argentina, Sir Henry Belfrage. When the ex-priest Rivas refers to pitying God Greene seems to be alluding, consciously or unconsciously, to Scobie's plight at the end of *The Heart of the Matter*. As in *A Burnt Out Case* and *The Comedians*, there are graphic accounts of the wretched lives of the insulted and injured of society, the poor and deprived in whose cause Rivas and his men are fighting. This is very effective journalistic writing, but it lacks the poetic intensity of the presentation of Mexico in *The Lawless Roads* and *The Power and the Glory*. Greene was much given in his fiction to scenes in which two characters talk or argue in a confined space, often at night, in near or complete darkness. There are several examples in *The Honorary Consul*; towards the end Plarr, Rivas and his men, and the captive consul are confined after dark in a hut which the police have surrounded. Rivas talks to the sceptical Plarr about his idea of God, an evolutionary concept in which the bright side of God is by degrees overcoming the dark side. This notion is probably derived from the controversial Jesuit theologian Pierre Teilhard de Chardin and seems to represent Greene's own position at that time. He believed, with some satisfaction, that it was rather heretical, but his attentive Spanish friend Father Durán assured him that, properly understood, such ideas are quite orthodox. Whether they are or not is irrelevant to the reader's response to the novel, a matter of theology rather than theology-in-fiction. In fact, Rivas's exposition is inert, adding nothing to the story; there is a telling contrast with *The Power and the Glory* where the whisky priest's painful attempts to maintain his relations with God have a strong dramatic function.* There is a lot of talk in *The Honorary Consul*, and quite a lot of action, some of it violent, but they are not related in any coherently dramatic fashion. The epigraph from Thomas Hardy is significant: 'All things merge into one another— good into evil, generosity into justice, religion into politics . . .' The weary tone of this is characteristic of the Greene Men, and so is the sentiment. In ordinary experience opposites may indeed merge into one another, but drama requires them to remain opposed. Greene's critical admirer David Lodge has remarked of this quotation, 'his most successful work was based on the clash of antithetical ideas rather than this hazy, ambiguous flow of one idea into another.'[4] This is true, and not only about ideas. In 1934 Greene had been fascinated by Frederick Rolfe opting for Hell if he could not have Heaven; in the Catholic novels of 1938–48 he presents characters who are very conscious of the difference between salvation and damnation: Pinkie, the whisky priest, Scobie. Readers may not have

---

* Greene claimed that the evolutionary concept of God was based on one of the many dreams that he carefully recorded in a diary. See *A World of My Own: a Dream Diary* (1992), 159–60.

believed in the religion and the dilemmas it imposed, but they recognized it as a powerful source of drama.

The Human Factor is Greene's first novel since 1951 to be set in England. It is backward-looking in several aspects. As a story about spies and secret agents it returns to the sources of his entertainments, as well as drawing on the personal wartime experience which he had satirically exploited in *Our Man in Havana*. We are once more in Berkhamsted, the scene of his boyhood experiences; in *The Lawless Roads* he had presented it as one of the anterooms of Hell, but *The Human Factor* gives it an air—ultimately illusory—of suburban comfort and regularity. The central figure of the novel, Maurice Castle, returns there every evening from his desk-job as an intelligence officer in St James's. He represents a recurring Greene motif in being a widower—his wife was killed in an air raid—who in middle age has married a young woman, Sarah, an educated and intelligent black South African. Castle fell in love with her when he was serving as a British agent in South Africa. She was under threat from the apartheid government and he helped her to escape with the aid of a local communist, now dead. They have married and live in Berkhamsted with Sarah's small son Sam, whom Castle, who has no children of his own, is very fond of; Sam's father, a black activist, is also dead. Castle has a guilty secret that Sarah does not know about: though a trusted employee of the secret service he is also, in a small way, a Soviet agent. This is not because of any ideological commitment to communism or the USSR—like most of Greene's principal characters he is a sceptic about ideologies—but because he believed that the communists were entitled to something in return for their help in getting Sarah out of South Africa. So he passes on little bits of information from time to time; he is on the point of winding up the connection, as he feels he has paid his debt to the Soviets. But such commitments are easier to get into than to get out of, and the novel shows the ensuing disintegration of the comfortable but frail world Castle and Sarah have made for themselves.

I have placed Castle as the last of the Greene Men, though with some hesitation. Like some of them, notably Querry, he has no friends or convictions and thinks of himself as a 'victim of loneliness and silence'. He tells a colleague, 'I haven't the faintest idea what the word "justice" means', echoing the sentiments of the Assistant Commissioner in *It's Battlefield*. The only value in his world comes from his love for his wife and stepson. He is so much of a hollow man that, as the phrase goes, we do not know what makes him tick, and it is this that separates him from the other Greene Men. As Roger Sharrock puts it in his discussion of *The Human Factor*: 'it is the divided, those at odds with the man within— Plarr, Brown, Querry, Fowler, Scobie—who enjoy the dubious luxury of a rich inner life.' This division is less evident in Castle; but he embodies the weariness that is a constant attribute of the others, and it is a quality that permeates the whole work, for *The Human Factor* is a tired narrative. At the end Castle is unmasked. Unlike many other Greene characters, he survives to the end of the novel, though death comes to one of his colleagues and his dog. But if he and Sarah are still alive, it is a life in death. Castle is spirited off to Moscow by the Russians; his wife wants to join him but she cannot take her son with her as he has not been entered on her passport and she will not be separated from him. It is a bleak and cruel conclusion. Greene wants to show the inherent and arbitrary cruelty in the modern world of *Realpolitik*, but some of the cruelty seems to be the author's own in his resolve to destroy the tenuous happiness of his characters.

Like other novels by Greene, *The Human Factor* has the appearance of a political novel, but without any real politics. Its plot was dependent on factors that seemed permanent features of the world at that time but have now disappeared: the Cold War and the apartheid regime in South Africa. It now looks merely remote, without having acquired a truly historical dimension. *The Human Factor* challenges plausibility at all levels, from the global to the personal. Castle ends up in permanent exile in Moscow, as had the Cambridge spies Guy Burgess and Donald Maclean, and Greene's friend Kim Philby. But they had been ideological believers in the communist cause, which Castle certainly is not. He betrays his country in order to return a favour; but then he does not believe that he has a country, other than his wife and her son. Roger Sharrock, who thinks better of the novel than I do, has commented pertinently on the question of motive:

> Greene's peculiar belief in the entirely private valuation of action, as if decisions were taken quite apart from group codes or inherited standards, means that his study of Maurice has no room to examine the tensions and conflicts we would normally associate with the life of a sensitive man acting as a double agent. Maurice is just a good ordinary man who happens to be found out.[5]

The Human Factor lacks credibility and conviction; Greene remarked of it in *Ways of Escape*, 'I am never satisfied with a novel, but I was more than usually dissatisfied with this one', and he was not wrong. Stories about secret agents may seem implausible and yet still work very effectively in their own terms, inviting a suspension of the reader's disbelief. I believe this is true of Greene's early entertainments; there is a sense in which *The Confidential Agent* offers the best possible critique of *The Human Factor*. Nevertheless, the latter presents interesting aspects if it is read against the grain, for hidden implications in the text rather than the development of the story. If Greene's most immediate model was the depressed and cynical story of secret agents in the Cold War as perfected by John le Carré, there is also a strong flavour of Buchan in the clubroom exchanges between the senior officials. They engage in much discussion of traditional English food, pondering the difference between steak and kidney pudding and steak and kidney pie. Dr Percival, a physician turned senior bureaucrat, believes that Lancashire hotpot is a safe choice on a menu, and is concerned with finding the best quality of smoked trout (he likes to catch trout as well as eat them and talks continually and boringly about trout fishing). He is a monster who, without quite meaning to, causes the death of Castle's assistant; in Greene's early novels he would have been more energetically and divertingly monstrous. Greene in his exile in the South of France seems to have been engaging in gastronomic nostalgia. There is a curious preoccupation with brand names of whisky in the novel, particularly J and B Rare, which Castle, who drinks more than his colleagues suspect, likes because it is a pale spirit that looks as if it has already been well diluted. References to this brand are frequent, in a form of product placement, the characters even referring to it by name as they pour out drinks, like people in a television commercial.

Greene's descriptions of London are perfunctory compared with his evocations of the 1930s. At the same time, he draws on his early work for motifs and situations. Sir John Hargreaves, head of the Intelligence Service, is an updated version of the Assistant Commissioner in *It's a Battlefield*; he has served in his early life as a District Commissioner in the Gold Coast and looks back longingly to his African experiences. There are some curious false notes. Two of the men at a lunch party given by Sir John are baffled by a reference to an 'ABC', popular teashops that have now vanished but were widespread for much of the twentieth century. The initials stood for 'Aereated Bread Company', but these officials claim never to have heard of these shops, though they were common enough for T. S. Eliot to refer to them in his poem 'A Cooking Egg', published in 1919. Greene may be engaging in a joke here, and elsewhere in the novel, but it remains a private joke. There is another puzzle in the way the names of Maurice and Sarah replicate those of the central characters in *The End of the Affair*, his last novel to be set in England.

NOTES

1. Norman Sherry, *The Life of Graham Greene*, III (London, 2004), 250, 384, 522.
2. Ibid. 154.
3. E. Waugh, *Diaries*, 779.
4. David Lodge, *The Practice of Writing* (London, 1996), 78.
5. R. Sharrock, *Saints, Sinners and Comedians* (Tunbridge Wells, 1984), 256.

8

Manic Interludes

In *Ways of Escape* Greene wrote, 'If *A Burnt Out Case* in 1961 represented the depressive side of a manic-depressive writer, *Travels with my Aunt* eight years later surely represented the manic at its height—or depth.' I would extend this comment to say that all the appearances of the Greene Man enacted the depressive side, with occasional incursions of the manic, as in the farcical episodes in *The Comedians*. The manic vein was already evident in some of Greene's writings of the 1950s, such as the light-hearted novella *Loser Takes All*, where an English accountant on his honeymoon in Monte Carlo finds a way of winning large sums at the gaming tables. Greene wrote it as a satirical but affectionate tribute to his friend Alexander Korda. This vein was then triumphantly expressed in a comic novel, *Our Man in Havana*. Greene called it an 'entertainment'; in the everyday sense of that word it is much more entertaining than *The Ministry of Fear*, his previous book in that subsequently abandoned category. The novel is set in Havana, in the final years of the Batista dictatorship; Greene later acknowledged that he had played down the violence and corruption of that playground for Western tourists. The central figure, James Wormold, is an expatriate Englishman who makes a modest living as the local agent for a company that manufactures vacuum cleaners. He has some of the attributes of the Greene Man, but he is too amiable and insufficiently tormented to be classed as one. Wormold has been married and divorced and is bringing up his daughter, Milly, to whom he is devoted. She loves her father, but has expensive tastes; a beautiful girl, 17 years old, a pious Catholic who attends a convent school, but with an entertainingly worldly side to her nature. She is one of Greene's few convincing female characters, who lights up the story when she appears. Milly is very likeable, but extravagant; she begs her father to buy her a pony, which he certainly cannot afford. Wormold's need to earn more money launches the narrative. He is approached one day in a bar by an unknown Englishman, an elegant silly ass who, we later learn, is an agent of the British intelligence service, based in Jamaica. His name is Henry Hawthorne; he bears one of Greene's recurring names, which has already made a momentary appearance near the beginning of the novel, when Wormold, trying to transact some business in a local American bank, has to wait while the clerk enjoys a lively telephone conversation with someone called Henry.

Hawthorne is trying to set up an intelligence network in the Caribbean and wants to recruit Wormold as a local agent. His work will be to provide information about developments in Cuba, in the light of the communist threat, which would become a reality a year or two later when Castro took over. To further this end he is to recruit local residents as sub-agents. Wormold is at first reluctant, fearing that he will be out of his depth in such activities, but he succumbs when he hears that the pay and expenses are generous. Greene had worked in the intelligence service during the war and in *Our Man in Havana* he looks at the system with a mocking, satirical eye. He shows Hawthorne's superiors in London as eager for any snatches of information and willing to pay for it. In the world of security any piece of information *might* be useful, so the desire for more and more information of any sort is incessant. At the top level there are considerations of departmental empire building, and a desire to outsmart the CIA, which is also active in Cuba. Wormold's problem, though, is that he has no information to provide and lacks the contacts to obtain it. He names, more or less at random, various Cubans of his acquaintance as sub-agents and receives allowances for them, though they have nothing to tell him. In desperation he starts inventing information and gets more and more caught up in the process. He makes sketches of parts of vacuum cleaners and claims that these are drawings of mysterious large installations that one of his agents has discovered in the mountains. His employers in London take it all very seriously and urge him to obtain photographs of the objects, which is a harder assignment.

At this satirical level *Our Man in Havana* is splendidly funny, revealing new capacities in Greene. But there is a further strand in the novel, which examines the nature of fiction itself. In a number of Greene's narratives there are novelists who reflect on their art and practice: Mr Savory in *Stamboul Train*, Maurice Bendrix in *The End of the Affair*, Jorge Julio Saavedra in *The Honorary Consul*. There are no novelists as such in *Our Man in Havana*, but Wormold turns into a virtual novelist, and a very imaginative and productive one. Nor is he the only one. Early in the story Hawthorne reports to his boss in London, the head of the intelligence service, known simply as the Chief. He is a severe figure, in a black morning coat with a black tie and a black monocle covering one eye. But he has a rich imagination and is ready not only to believe what Hawthorne tells him about Wormold but to elaborate it in novelistic fashion, establishing him as a character:

'you understand it's not a big office, sir. Old fashioned. You know how these merchant-adventurers make do.'

'I know the type, Hawthorne. Small scrubby desk. Half a dozen men in an outer office meant to hold two. Out-of-date accounting machines. Woman-secretary who is completing forty years with the firm.'

Hawthorne now felt able to relax; the Chief had taken charge. Even if one day he read the secret file, the words would convey nothing to him.

The small shop for vacuum cleaners had been drowned beyond recovery in the tide of the Chief's literary imagination. Agent 59200/5 was established. (part 1, 'Interlude in London')

The Chief continues to develop his confident account of the agent's character as an old-fashioned, lonely loyalist: 'Our man in Havana belongs to the Kipling age.' It is a delightfully comic exchange. Like the Chief, Wormold is a dedicated storyteller and he has more opportunities to exercise the art. Early in his new career he explains it to Milly:

When Milly came home that evening he was still busy, writing his first report with a large map of Cuba spread over his desk.
   'What are you doing, Father?'
   'I am taking the first step in a new career.'
   She looked over his shoulder. 'Are you becoming a writer?'
   'Yes, an imaginative writer.'
   'Will you earn a lot of money?'
   'A moderate income, Milly, if I set my mind to it and write regularly. I plan to compose an essay like this every Saturday evening.' (part 2, ch. 3)

The London headquarters send out an assistant-cum-minder called Beatrice to work with Wormold. Before she knows what he is up to she tells him that he talks like a novelist, treating his agents like 'people in a book'. In time Wormold starts to weary of his characters: 'He was tempted to call out to all his creations at once and have done with them.'

Then the so-called real world impinges on his fictional one. Havana is full of spies, and the agents of another power—we are never told which—are intercepting Wormold's messages and start trying to eliminate his alleged contacts, which is hard on them as they know nothing about their role in his fictions. The action turns into an espionage drama that is violent as well as farcical; as Beatrice remarks, 'We're back into the *Boy's Own Paper* world.' It was a world that had long been familiar to Greene. The fictional order that Wormold had carefully built up starts disintegrating, though the Chief in London continues to believe in him—after all, he has in a sense invented Wormold—and even recommends him for an OBE and holds out the prospect of another job. Wormold has fallen in love with Beatrice, who is rather a nullity as a character, and they intend to marry. She decides that she no longer wants to work in secret intelligence, and so does he. At the end of the novel Wormold and Milly and Beatrice have left Cuba and are preparing to face an uncertain future in England.

Our Man in Havana shows Greene's ability to set novels in parts of the world that soon afterwards become crisis centres. This was true of *A Burnt Out Case*, located in the Belgian Congo shortly before it became independent and collapsed into civil war. In 1959, the year after Greene's Cuban novel was published, Castro came to power, swept away the Batista regime, and began a permanent state of frozen conflict in his country's relations with the United States. Greene's later sympathies were with Castro but *Our Man in Havana* is not a political novel. As Greene acknowledged, it takes a simplified and simplifying view of its corrupt setting, but that is the sort of thing comic writing does. In this novel Greene's manic impulses were controlled and directed with a light touch, and the result is highly accomplished comedy, at a level that he never reached again.

Greene's next comic novel, written out of his manic vein, is *Travels with My Aunt*. It is what novel reviewers like to call a 'romp', tracing rapid picaresque adventures across the world. The story is narrated by Henry Pulling, the first of Greene's central characters to bear that trademark name since Henry Scobie. In the opening pages he is at his mother's funeral, in the fourth cremation in Greene's novels. Henry is the apotheosis of the dim bourgeois, a middle-aged retired bank manager who has never married and whose only interest in life is growing dahlias. At the funeral he meets his mother's younger sister Aunt Augusta, who has had little contact with the family. Aunt Augusta is colourful, dashing, and wealthy. She decides that Henry needs a change of scene and she whisks him off to foreign parts. The story goes energetically on from there, in a spirit of rapid improvisation. In some episodes Greene is deliberately alluding to his own earlier writings; there is a visit to Brighton, and a journey to Istanbul on the Orient Express, which has come down in the world since Greene wrote about it in *Stamboul Train*. A recurring figure in Aunt Augusta's life is Visconti, a con man and alleged war criminal, who is known as 'the viper' by his enemies. Greene is reminding us of the villain of that name in Marjorie Bowen's *The Viper of Milan*, the historical romance that he read with absorption in his youth, and which contributed to his personal mythology. Other motifs occur from his early writings; there are references to a girl called Rose, and to a woman named Rosa. Other echoes of earlier passages may be inadvertent. On board a river steamer in Argentina Henry has to submit to having his palm read, just as Wilson does in *The Heart of the Matter*. Henry is briefly imprisoned in Paraguay—the South American episodes in this novel suggest an early draft for *The Honorary Consul*—and the description recalls the priest's imprisonment in *The Power and the Glory*: 'There was nothing to sit on in the cell—only a piece of sacking under a barred window too high for me to see anything but a patch of monotonous sky. Somebody had written on the wall in Spanish—perhaps a prayer, perhaps an obscenity, I couldn't tell.' Far too often Henry Pulling is no more than a stylistic mouthpiece for his author, as when he reflects, 'My responsibility was over, but she stayed on in my memory like a small persistent pain which worries even in its insignificance; doesn't a sickness as serious as cancer start in such a way?'; or 'Anxieties in his case would always settle on him like flies on an open wound'. Pulling sounds like Greene, and Greene sounds as if he is unconsciously parodying himself; unless—and one cannot rule it out—Greene the joker is up to some self-referring trickery. *Travels with My Aunt* presents itself as something original in Greene's career, but it is permeated with what he has written before.

Henry Pulling tells the story, but the rakish and overbearing Aunt Augusta, who is a lively old girl in her seventies, controls the action. Her surname, incidentally, is Bertram, which was that of the narrator of *Loser Takes All*, though this is a connection without any obvious point. Aunt Augusta, we learn, makes her money by currency smuggling. She combines the tone and manner of Lady Bracknell with what sounds like a vivid past as a *grande horizontale*. She has a lover cum personal servant, a black man called Wordsworth, though she is trying to get rid of him. Aunt Augusta is a female version of those lords of misrule who wander through European literature, overturning the lives of those she meets. At the end of the novel Henry has started learning about life. He has made a surprising discovery about his parentage, and is settling down to a new career in Paraguay with Aunt Augusta and Visconti, and the prospect of marriage to the 16-year-old daughter of the Chief of Customs.

Greene was clearly enraptured with Aunt Augusta, and expected his readers to be, but I must confess I find her unutterably tedious; similarly, Wordsworth, the cheerful Mr Fixit with the patter of a stage darkie (I doubt if Greene could get away with such a character if he were writing today). Wordsworth shares the fate of other Greene characters by being killed off in the final pages. *Travels with My Aunt* would provide an entertaining read on a train journey or a short flight, but it is too manic by half. Greene wrote only one successful comic novel.

9

Last Words

IN the 1980s Greene published two short novels in a fabular vein, *Doctor Fischer of Geneva or the Bomb Party* and *Monsignor Quixote*, which led his fiction in new directions. After a long immersion in anomic tropical regions, we are transported in *Doctor Fischer* to the cold clean air, civic amenity, and Protestant austerity of Switzerland: Greeneland's icy mountains, in short. The narrator, Alfred Jones, has a very common English surname, previously borne by one of the central trio in *The Comedians*. At the start of the novel he is a lonely middle-aged widower whose wife has died in childbirth, together with their baby daughter. He lives in Switzerland, using his linguistic skills in a humble job translating foreign correspondence for a manufacturer of chocolate. He lost his left hand when fighting fires in the London Blitz, and is self-conscious about this deformity. He finds unexpected happiness after a casual meeting with Anna-Luise, the young daughter of the eponymous Doctor Fischer, a toothpaste tycoon; despite the difference in their ages, she and Jones fall in love and marry. (The January–May marriage is a recurring motif in late Greene, as with Charley Fortnum and Teresa, and Maurice Castle and Sarah). Anna-Luise hates her father for having driven her mother into an early grave, and Fischer is well worth hating; Jones's first words are, 'I think that I used to detest Doctor Fischer more than any man I have known just as I loved his daughter more than any other woman.'

Fischer is a rich monster who uses his great wealth to torment a circle of flattering toadies who have hopes of inheriting some of it; Anna-Luise, whose English is imperfect, thinks that Jones has called them 'toads', and this is how he refers to them for the rest of the novel. They comprise a lawyer, a tax consultant, an army officer, a superannuated film star, and, the only female among them, a gushing American woman. They are the regular dinner guests of Doctor Fischer, who amuses himself by humiliating and insulting them throughout the meal; they put up with this because of the lavish gifts they will receive at the end of it. This is a motif from the grimmer kinds of folklore; it also suggests a reversal of the plot of *Volpone*; in Jonson's play the rich manipulator pretends to be dying so as to extract gifts from the toadies, each of them hoping to be his heir. Doctor Fischer humiliates his greedy followers even more by giving them luxury goods that they do not need. Fischer is quite indifferent to his daughter and to her marriage, but he wants to see what sort of man Jones is and invites him to his next dinner party. There Fischer is served with caviare, and the guests are given plates of cold porridge, which they are expected to eat in the hope of rewards to come. Jones refuses to eat any, and so earns Fischer's respect. Fischer is referred to as acting like God in his manipulation of people's lives; he is happy to accept this parallel, though he does not believe in God; he remarks, 'judging from the world he is supposed to have made, he can only be greedy for our humiliation...'* Fischer pursues this idea by saying that God sometimes gives people presents to compensate for the customary humiliation of their lives: 'For example, you are a poor man, so he gives you a small present, my daughter, to keep you satisfied a little longer.'

---

* There are interesting parallels between Greene's novel and Terry Southern's *The Magic Christian* (1959), where the manipulative tycoon Guy Grand ('a grand guy') sets up elaborate practical jokes that baffle and humiliate large numbers of people. Fischer concentrated on a small circle of sycophants, whereas Guy Grand's potential target was the whole population of the United States.

Jones is more than satisfied; his marriage with Anna-Luise is one of the few happy unions in Greene's oeuvre. But it is no surprise to learn that it cannot last; Anna-Luise is abruptly removed from the scene by being killed in a skiing accident (it is a shocking episode, reminiscent of the way in which E. M. Forster wrote a character out of *The Longest Journey*, 'Gerald died that afternoon, broken up on the football field').

Doctor Fischer is a figure of ingenious and towering malignity—he recalls the energetic grotesques in Greene's early novels—who gets repeated entertainment from tormenting the toadies. He has no feelings about his daughter's death but he tells Jones he will make him rich if he will only fit in with Fischer's plans; Jones, too, he believes will become a grasping toad in the end: 'I shall have created you. Just as much as God created Adam.' Fischer here sounds not only like God but like a pseudo-novelist, creating characters just as Wormold had done. But after Anna-Luise's death, Jones does not want to live, and he thinks he can take advantage of a final spectacular event that Fischer has planned in order to end his life. On this occasion there is a great banquet with fine food and wine for everyone; though it is midwinter it takes place out of doors, but the cold is kept off by great bonfires. Once again the guests will receive presents after the meal, but this time with a difference. Previously Fischer had not engaged in the ultimate humiliation of giving his guests money, rather than expensive presents; this time, though, each will receive a cheque for a very large sum. But there is a catch in it: the cheques will be concealed in Christmas crackers, in one of which there will not be a cheque but a possibly lethal explosive device. It is a form of Russian roulette, the deadly game which Greene claimed to have played in his youth. The guests are greedy enough to take a chance and several of them successfully pull a cracker and safely extract a cheque. Jones does not want a cheque, but he does want to die and he believes that pulling the explosive cracker will be a good way of committing suicide. When the other crackers have been pulled he takes the remaining one; an oddity about this game is that the guests pull the crackers by themselves, rather than with other people as is usually the case. Jones has to do it awkwardly, as he has only one effective hand; he puts one end in his mouth and pulls the other. And nothing happens; Fischer has lied to his guests in order to complete their humiliation. At the end of the novel it is not Jones who is dead, but Fischer; he retreats from the warm illuminated circle into the darkness, and shoots himself. He joins that succession of Greene characters who end up lifeless on the ground in the final pages: Querry, Wordsworth, Plarr, Rivas. Jones remarks, 'I looked at the body and it had no more significance than a dead dog. This, I thought, was the bit of rubbish I had once compared in my mind with Jehovah and Satan.' Jones does not commit suicide; he returns to the humdrum life he been living at the opening of the story, sustained by memories of Anna-Luise.

The quality of the writing suggests that a new setting and a new genre had revivified Greene, for it has a freshness and sharpness frequently lacking in the narratives of the Greene Man; the description of the final Bomb Party has a dream-like vividness. But *Doctor Fischer* is a puzzling work. It has been interpreted as a satire on the rich, or a parable about human greed, but such accounts seem to me to limit its originality. It reads like a dream narrative, particularly in such inconsequential details as Jones's missing hand, which has no obvious point or relevance. Indeed, it may have had its origin in the dreams which Greene carefully recorded in a special diary, a selection from which was posthumously published in *A World of My Own*. Greene could well have been happy to puzzle his readers, mildly tormenting them about what he was up to, just as Fischer subjected his guests to worse torments. If *Doctor Fischer* had burst upon the world as the first book of a new and unknown novelist, it would, I think, have been appreciated for its sharp prose, the

perverse ingenuity of the story, the contemptible toads, the fascinating nastiness of Fischer, and the contrasting pathos in the love of
Jones and Anna-Luise. I could imagine it being described as a work
of considerable accomplishment and great promise. But promise is
not a quality one can ascribe to a novelist who has been working—
and living—for as long as Greene had in 1980.

The new fabular vein was continued in *Monsignor Quixote*, which
is set in Spain. Among other things, this novel is an essay in intertextuality, which proposes that all literature to some extent draws
on other literature, whether by imitating it, continuing it, or parodying it. Greene's model is suggested by his title; he presents the
adventures of a latter day Don Quixote and Sancho Panza travelling
through modern Spain, and the book is modelled on Cervantes'
great original, even down to the chapter headings. The eponymous
central character is said to be a descendant of the original Don
Quixote, though he himself is a humble country priest; his bishop
resents this distinguished ancestry and echoes the potential scepticism of the reader by asking, 'How can he be descended from a fictional character?' But we have to believe it. Father Quixote's
fortunes are changed by a simple act of charity to a passing
stranger; in this case, an Italian bishop of rather grand aspect whose
Mercedes has broken down. Quixote provides him with lunch and
wine, and even mends the bishop's car for him. The bishop, who
turns out to be a high Vatican official, is effusively grateful, and tells
Father Quixote that he is made for better things than life as an
obscure country priest. He thinks no more of it, but a few weeks
later he receives a cross letter from his own bishop, telling him that
for some inexplicable reason the Holy Father has advanced Quixote
to the rank of Monsignor, on the recommendation of the visiting
Italian ecclesiastic. The bishop has long disapproved of Quixote,
not only for his ancestry, but for having once imprudently sup-
ported a radical charity. He tells Monsignor Quixote, as he now is,

that it will not be appropriate for him to stay in his present humble post and he will take steps to have him moved elsewhere, the further the better. This will take time, and meanwhile he encourages Quixote to go off on a vacation; a young priest of unquestioned orthodoxy will be put in temporary charge of the parish.

Quixote takes to the road, following in the steps of his ancestor, in his battered Seat car which he calls Rocinante, the name of Don Quixote's horse. The story demands that he has a companion, and this is the communist mayor of the village, who has just been turned out of office in an election. His name is Zancas, which was the name of the original Sancho Panza, and Quixote teases him by calling him Sancho. The two men are ideological opponents but good friends who enjoy argument, chipping away at each other's beliefs. The careers of both of them have been overturned, and they agree to take a holiday together. *Monsignor Quixote* is a charming story, and charm is not a quality one often finds in Greene's writing. The journeys it describes are drawn from the trips through Spain that Greene took with his Spanish friend Father Leopoldo Durán, as described in the latter's memoir of Greene. Father Durán denies that he had anything to do with the character of Monsignor Quixote; it is true that he was a university professor rather than a country priest, but to judge from his memoir both he and Greene's character regarded the world in similarly naïve and innocent ways. (Greene complicated the issue by introducing a Father Leopoldo at the end of the novel, but he is a Trappist monk.) Writing dialogue, which Greene did well, is a familiar way of filling up the pages of a novel, and there is a great deal of talk in the first part of *Monsignor Quixote* as the travellers drive along the roads of Spain. There are elements of the fictional travelogue. Quixote and Sancho visit the grandiose tomb that Franco had built for himself, and the house in Salamanca where the quasi-Catholic philosopher Miguel de Unamuno had died; as a student, Sancho had attended his lectures when he was still a Catholic, and jokingly blames him for keeping him in the Church too long. Unamuno was a great devotee of Don Quixote, and his famous book *The Tragic Sense of Life* was one of Greene's intellectual points of reference in his later years.

During the conversations between Quixote and Sancho they discover that their respective faiths in Catholicism and communism are less than absolute, based on hope as much as certainty, whatever they profess in their public roles. There is both a parallel, and a striking contrast, between their discussions and that between the priest and the atheistic police lieutenant in *The Power and the Glory*, which marked an absolute division between opposed attitudes to the world, the religious, and the secular-humanist. (There are allusions to this novel in *Monsignor Quixote*; the hero refuses another drink, saying that he does not want to be regarded as a 'whisky priest', and later says that his only relation is a second cousin who is a priest in Mexico.) As Lodge has pointed out, in his later career Greene tended to see opposites as joining and blurring, which means an increase in general good will but a slackening of dramatic tension. Greene presents both Catholicism and communism as worthy causes with an embarrassing history.

There is gentle humour as well as charm in *Monsignor Quixote*, as, for instance, in the comic episode when the shabby priest goes to a posh ecclesiastical outfitters in Madrid—probably run by Opus Dei, it is suggested—in order to buy socks in monseigneural purple. There is amiable satire on traditional Catholic practices in the description of the advice and opinions contained in a standard textbook on moral theology. Quixote notes that though there are fifteen references to Hell in St Mathew's Gospel, there are none at all in St John's. When a narrowly orthodox priest says that surely he is not questioning the existence of Hell, Quixote responds 'I believe from obedience, but not with the heart'. The discussions in *Monsignor Quixote* are enlightening, entertaining, and sometimes funny. But it takes more than talk to make a novel, as Greene realizes, and in the latter part of the book he inserts some violent action, involving Quixote and Sancho in adventures paralleling those of the original pair. The story speeds up and in the process loses its serenity and balance. Quixote, out of charity, helps an escaped prisoner to get away from the pursuing Civil Guard and henceforth he and Sancho are on the wrong side of the law. His bishop suspends him from his priestly functions, and makes what he regards as the charitable assumption that Quixote has had a mental breakdown. At the end of the novel one is inclined to think that the bishop may be right. Quixote and Sancho are driving to a Trappist monastery where they hope to find sanctuary. Just as they reach it the pursuing police catch up with them and shoot the tyres out of the car. It crashes; Sancho and Quixote are shaken but not badly hurt, and the monks take them into the monastery to rest and recover. But Quixote does not recover. The loss of his role as a priest has led to a loss of his purpose in life, and of his sense of reality. He wanders sleepwalking through the monastery, and begins to say Mass, without bread and wine and chalice, though he acts as if they were there. Then he collapses and dies; it is the common fate of Greene's protagonists, though it is a gentler death than most of them undergo. And it provides a parallel to the edifying demise of the original Don Quixote in the final pages of Cervantes' book.

Looked at one way, *Monsignor Quixote* represents a fresh start by an aged but still enterprising author; looked at another way it marks the end of Greene's lifelong affair with the art of the novel, almost a Prospero's farewell. But it was not quite the end. In 1985 a novella unpublished for more than forty years appeared before the public, like an archaeological fragment that had worked its way to the surface of the ground. This was *The Tenth Man*, which Greene had written in 1944 as the outline for a film set in wartime France under the German occupation. The material was never used and it lay forgotten in the archives of a film company until it was eventually discovered and published. It is a vintage Greene narrative, with the familiar themes of betrayal and pursuit and deception. A number of hostages in a prison are to be shot by the Nazis; one of them, a prosperous lawyer, persuades another prisoner to take his place, in exchange for his country house and all his wealth. This man agrees, and before he is shot makes a will leaving everything to his mother and sister. After his release from prison the lawyer, now penniless, makes his way to what was once his ancestral home and meets the dead man's sister. *The Tenth Man* is a powerful story that makes good use of the folklore motif of the doppelgänger when a stranger turns up and claims to be the real survivor. In his introduction to the rediscovered novella Greene said that he found it very readable, and was inclined to prefer it to his more famous piece of fiction written for the cinema, *The Third Man*. I think he was right on both counts. Another fragment of fiction derived from Greene's work in film in the early 1950s was published in 2005 as a 15,000-word novella, *No Man's Land*. It sets out the story for a proposed film to be made with Carol Reed as a follow-up to the highly successful *Third Man*. Like that work it deals with the early days of clashes between East and West in Central Europe. It is a spy story set in the Harz Mountains in Germany, with a strong love interest that anticipates the obsessive concern with betrayal and jealousy that pervade *The End of the Affair*. There is a strong Catholic element, focused on a rather improbable Marian shrine in the mountains. The novella is a curiosity rather than a work of high literary significance; the film was never made, apparently because Reed thought, with some reason, that Greene's treatment was merely repeating devices and motifs from *The Third Man* (and Greene himself appeared to be losing interest in it).

Greene's career as a novelist ended in 1988 with *The Captain and the Enemy*. One wishes he had gone out with a stronger book. For a long time his novels had been recycling material from his life, or types and episodes and motifs from his earlier fiction. This is abundantly true of *The Captain and the Enemy*; it opens in an unnamed but recognizable Berkhamsted; much of the middle part of the novel takes place in a basement flat in Camden Town, which recalls the one where D. found refuge in *The Confidential Agent*, and, before that, the setting for Greene's haunting short story 'The Basement Room'. The last part of *The Captain and the Enemy* returns to Latin America and the regions of the mind that had fascinated him ever since his visit to Mexico in 1938. It ends in Panama, a country Greene became familiar with towards the end of his life, as he describes in *Getting to Know the General*, his admiring account of its president, General Torrijos.

Despite his initial difficulties with first-person narrative in *The End of the Affair*, Greene used it freely in subsequent novels, and most of *The Captain and the Enemy* is narrated by Victor Baxter; at the beginning, he is a boy at a public school, where he is bullied and unhappy. He has reason to be; his mother is dead and his father takes no interest in him beyond paying his school bills, and has passed the boy over to an unsympathetic aunt to bring up. Victor's life is transformed when one day a genial stranger arrives at the school, claiming to be a friend of his father, from whom he brings a letter to the headmaster, asking permission for the boy to be taken out for the afternoon. This leave is granted and the man takes Victor to lunch in a local pub, which he contrives not to pay for. He likes to be known as the Captain, though he goes through life under many different names and titles. He is one of Greene's favourite types, the con man or trickster, who first appears as Anthony Farrant in *England Made Me* and was further developed as Jones in *The Comedians*. The Captain asks Victor if he really wants to go back to school after the outing; if he does they will go to the cinema and then the Captain will return the boy. When Victor says he would be happy not to return to school the Captain acts instantly and they take a train to London. A folklore element becomes dominant when the Captain explains that he has won Victor in a game with his hard-hearted father, though whether at backgammon or chess remains unclear. Victor has in effect been kidnapped, though with his consent; he hates his school and likes the Captain and is ready for a new life.

This life is lived in a basement flat in London, where his companion is a harassed young woman called Lisa, whom the Captain wants him to call Mother. In time it emerges that Lisa had been seduced by Victor's father and made to have an abortion after she became pregnant. She mourns the loss of her child, and the Captain, who had been a friend of Baxter senior, resolves to replace it with Baxter's own unwanted son, which is why Victor has become a stake in a game. The Captain does not live with Lisa in the basement flat, but comes and goes in an unpredictable way. They do not appear to be lovers, though she is evidently devoted to him; his feeling for her is paternal, or so it seems. There is an ambiguity about the relationship which is never resolved; the Captain is one of Greene's recurring types, and Lisa is another, the struggling waif. The Captain does not like Victor's Christian name, and decides to call him Jim. This was the name of Wormold in *Our Man in Havana* (and of Conrad's flawed hero); the Captain's original name, we learn, was Brown, which is familiar in Greene's oeuvre. He is away for long periods, but he ensures there is enough money for Jim to be educated.

The first part of the novel has the air of romance or fable. It is an air that Jim, who has read *King Solomon's Mines* four times, enjoys breathing. In the next part he has grown up, has become a journalist, and wants to write fiction. He looks back in later life at his dealings with the Captain and Lisa with the cool eye of a Greeneian novelist, 'It is as though I had taken them quite coldbloodedly as fictional characters to satisfy this passionate desire of mine to write.'

The Captain suddenly comes back in Jim's life. He receives a letter from him, containing a plane ticket to Panama, and an urgent invitation to join him there; he holds out the prospect of a great adventure that will make a good deal of money. Jim is bored with his dead-end job on a local paper and accepts the invitation. The rest of the novel, set in the Central American republic, has affinities with Greene's recent fiction, and is in a mode of depressed realism, describing violence and political intrigue, but it also recalls the boys' adventure stories that had been one of his early literary resources. The Captain is now known as Mr Smith, and is engaged in an idealistic adventure, smuggling arms to the guerrillas fighting the Somoza dictatorship in Nicaragua.

Greene regularly made references or allusions to his earlier novels; this seems to be the case when a sinister character called Mr Quigly, who claims to be a journalist but is really a CIA agent, refers to his British birth: 'Born in Brighton. You can't be more English than that.' Elsewhere it is not clear whether we are faced with deliberate self-reference or unconscious self-imitation; when Jim writes, 'I backed towards the door and threw the truth at him like a glass of vitriol', we may or may not be meant to think of Pinkie's violent end. The adult Jim readily drops into the sententious tones of a Greene Man: 'Each love affair was like a vaccine. It helped you to get through the next attack more easily.' The brief concluding section of the novel is told in the third person, and describes the fate of the principal characters, which is on predictable lines. Lisa has already been killed in a road accident in London. The Captain dies in a plane crash, and Jim is killed in an accident on the way to the airport when he is about to fly out of the country; the Panamanian officer who reports this news in the final paragraph adds, 'If it was really an accident, which I doubt'. The CIA have disposed of Jim, we assume. *The Captain and the Enemy* reassembles constituents that had preoccupied Greene throughout his career, and the result is, as it always was, very readable. He had nothing more to say, but he said it very professionally.

This novel was not Greene's final appearance as a writer of fiction in his lifetime, for in 1990 he published *The Last Word and Other Stories*, a slender volume of 150 well-spaced pages and a corresponding insubstantiality in the contents; indeed, it is an exercise in scraping the barrel. The stories cover the whole of Greene's career. The first, a cynical little fable called 'The New House', dates from 1923 when he was an undergraduate. The last, dated 1989, anticipated the ceremonial opening of the Channel Tunnel and described how it was blown up by terrorists. Greene was wrong about that occasion; one hopes that his well-known prescience will not be justified at some point in the future. His introduction to the collection suggests the leg-puller at work. He says, for instance, that his reason for reprinting a contrived murder-story written in 1929 is that when he reread it he had no idea who the murderer was. This was not the spirit in which, early in his career, Greene suppressed two whole novels because he felt they were not up to standard. The point of this collection, I believe, was that it gave Greene the opportunity to publish a book called *The Last Word*, and to die the following year.

After the novelist's last word, comes the critic's. A study such as this does not lend itself to a pithy rounding off, or a QED. I believe that Greene's career as a novelist shows a pattern evident in the lives of many writers, and indeed other kinds of artist. There is an opening phase marked by formal originality, imaginative vitality, and strength of feeling. It may also be marred by inexperience, by an inadequate sense of form, and by excess of ambition. The phase of maturity shows mastery of the medium, but combined with a certain loss of the early freshness and energy. In Greene's novels of the 1930s and 1940s what I see as his strengths are evident, as well as some of the weaknesses. They are not realistic novels, though they contain starkly realistic episodes; they are fables or romances, and they are poetic and melodramatic. They show Greene's capacity for polyphonic or multi-tracked writing; what initially reads like a thriller will embody qualities of both poetry and realism; and it is likely to contain a tissue of literary allusions. The prose is both fast-moving and metaphorical. The process culminates in Greene's masterpiece *Brighton Rock*, and it can be summed up in the remark of Allott and Ferris that as a writer Greene is closer to Webster than to Thackeray.

Writers move on, and very long-lived ones can move a long way. Greene reacted against the elaborate manner of his opening phase, and aimed at a simpler, more direct mode of writing. This became evident in the 1950s, when he published three novels of high quality, of sharply contrasting kinds: *The End of the Affair*, the last of his Catholic novels and the last for many years to be set in England (which he had once believed was the proper setting for his fiction), and *The Quiet American* and *Our Man in Havana*, which opened up overseas provinces of Greeneland. Thereafter Greene wrote a series of novels with a plain narrative line, where the occasional metaphors seem added and intrusive. These books were vehicles for the Greene Man; they were skilfully written and constructed, thrilling and suspenseful; and they contain enough mordant reflections about life and death to provide an intermittent air of profundity. They pleased readers throughout the world, and Greene became one of the few English writers of the twentieth century to achieve a global reputation. Nevertheless, I think they are not his best work. This is not what is widely believed about Greene, if one may judge from the centenary celebrations of 2004, so it is a relief to find others are of the same mind. Some remarks in a private communication to me by the American religious columnist (and Orthodox priest) John Garvey effectively sum up my position, 'Greene was always a good read, but there is nothing in the later stuff like the darkness at the heart of *Brighton Rock* . . . The sad thing is that a person capable of *Brighton Rock*, instead of going deeper, became competent at a kind of genre writing, as if the young Dostoevsky turned into Raymond Chandler. Nothing wrong with Chandler, but it is a devolution.'

I have previously quoted David Lodge's reservations about Greene's later fiction. He has acknowledged Greene's influence on his own early novels, and in *The British Museum is Falling Down* (1966) he makes it explicit in a witty parody. One of the characters in a later novel, *How Far Can You Go?* (1980), is a young academic who is writing a thesis on Greene, and the progress of the narrative through the 1950s and 1960s is punctuated by the appearance of fresh novels by him. Writing after Greene's death, Lodge reaffirmed his belief that Greene's novels and entertainments of the 1930s and 1940s 'up to and including *The End of the Affair*, were the work of a major writer, without which the map of modern literary history would look significantly different'. But he goes on to say of *The Comedians, Travels with My Aunt, The Honorary Consul*, and *The Human Factor*, 'Never less than technically accomplished, these novels are in the end curiously unsatisfying because they pick up large political and philosophical issues only to drop them unresolved.'[1] More recently he has described Greene's literary career as 'a story of the gradual decline of creative power from a very high peak of achievement'.[2] There is a similar judgement in the memoir of Greene by his friend Shirley Hazzard:

The inspired pain of the earlier fiction would not recur; or even the intensity of those lighter and livelier works that Graham had once differentiated as 'entertainments'. What remained was professionalism: a unique view and tone, a practised, topical narrative that held the interest and forced the pace of the reader. Poignancy was largely subsumed into world-weariness, resurfacing in spasms of authenticity. In the later work, sheer human sympathy makes an obligatory guest appearance, like an ageing celebrity briefly brought on stage.[3]

There is nothing here that I would want to alter, and nothing that I could put as well. An attempt at revaluation, such as I have undertaken, is liable in our excitable literary climate to be regarded as an 'attack' and welcomed or condemned accordingly. That is not what I intended; I hope people will go on reading Greene, but read him rather differently, and perhaps read him better.

NOTES

1. D. Lodge, *The Practice of Writing* (London, 1996), 78–9.
2. Review of Sherry, iii, *New York Review of Books*, 2 December 2004.
3. S. Hazzard, *Greene on Capri* (London, 2000), 57–8.

BOOKS BY GRAHAM GREENE

(This is not a completely comprehensive list, but mentions books referred to or discussed. For a full account of Greene's publications up to the 1970s see R. A. Wobbe, *Graham Greene, A Bibliography and Guide to Research*, New York, 1979.)

Novels and Novellas

The Man Within, 1929
The Name of Action, 1930
Rumour at Nightfall, 1931
Stamboul Train, 1932
It's a Battlefield, 1934
England Made Me, 1935
A Gun for Sale, 1936
Brighton Rock, 1938
The Confidential Agent, 1939
The Power and the Glory, 1940
The Ministry of Fear, 1943
The Heart of the Matter, 1948
The Third Man, 1950
The End of the Affair, 1951
The Quiet American, 1954
Loser Takes All, 1955
Our Man in Havana, 1958
A Burnt Out Case, 1961
The Comedians, 1966
Travels with My Aunt, 1969
The Honorary Consul, 1973
The Human Factor, 1978

Doctor Fischer of Geneva or the Bomb Party, 1980
Monsignor Quixote, 1982
The Tenth Man, 1985
The Captain and the Enemy, 1988
No Man's Land, 2005

Short Stories

Collected Stories, 1972
The Last Word and Other Stories, 1990

Plays

Collected Plays, 1985

Essays and Journalism

British Dramatists, 1942
Collected Essays, 1969
Reflections, 1990
Articles of Faith, 2006

Writings on Film

The Pleasure Dome, 1972
Mornings in the Dark, 1993

Travel Writings

Journey Without Maps, 1936
The Lawless Roads, 1939
In Search of a Character, 1961
Getting to Know the General, 1984

Autobiographies

A Sort of Life, 1971
Ways of Escape, 1980
A World of My Own, 1992

INDEX

(Extended discussions are indicated in bold type)

91, 112, 114, 169, 172; *The Tenth
Man* 142, **181–2**; *The Third
Man* 125, 142, 182; *Travels with
my Aunt* 18, 19, 72, **171–3**, 188
(Short Stories) *The Last Word*
186; *May We Borrow Your
Husband?* 19; 'The Basement
Room' 43, 183; 'A Drive in the
Country' 42; 'The End of the
Party' 41; 'The New House'
186; 'A Visit to Morin' 149–51
(Plays) *Carving a Statue* 19; *The
Great Jowett* 17; *The Living
Room* 16, 66; *The Potting Shed*
18, 19, 148; *Yes and No* 17
(Essays) *British Dramatists* 16,
58, 90–1; *Essais Catholiques*
137; 'Frederick Rolfe:
Edwardian Inferno' 92;
'Henry James: the Religious
Aspect' 92–3, 137, 139
(Travel Writings) *Getting to
Know the General* 183; *In
Search of a Character* 106, 115,
153; *The Lawless Roads* 15, 94,
103–10, 115, 145, 151, 160–2
(Autobiographies) *A Sort of Life*
91; *Ways of Escape* 75, 93, 97,
110, 124, 136, 150, 167; *A World
of My Own* 177
(Edited work) *The Old School* 49
Gregor, Ian 125, 132–3
Griffith, D. W. 29–30

Haggard, Henry Rider 23; *King
Solomon's Mines* 184
Hamilton, Patrick 88

Hanley, James, *No Directions* 75
Hardy, Thomas 28, 30, 161
Hazzard, Shirley 97, 188
Hemingway, Ernest, *For Whom the
Bell Tolls* 115
Hitchcock, Alfred 31, 77
Honegger, Arthur 28
Hoggart, Richard, *The Uses of
Literacy* 44
Hopkins, Gerard 135
Huxley, Aldous 24

James, Henry 23, 33, 41, 85, 92–3,
125; *The Wings of the Dove* 49;
'The Altar of the Dead' 93;
'The Turn of the Screw' 41,
93
Jonson, Ben 26, 33, 175; *Volpone*
175
Joyce, James 39, 47; *Ulysses* 47

Kermode, Frank 129, 133
Kinglake, A. W. 37
Knox, Ronald 140
Koestler, Arthur, *Darkness at Noon*
158
Korda, Alexander 167
Kreuger, Ivar 47–8

Lang, Fritz 77
Lawrence, D. H. 22
le Carré, John 22
Lodge, David 25, 28, 30, 123,
128–9, 161, 180, 187; *The
British Museum is Falling
Down* 188; *How Far Can You
Go?* 123, 188